# A Kid's Guide to
# CREATING
# WEB PAGES

## for Home and School

# A Kid's Guide to

# CREATING WEB PAGES

## for Home and School

**Benjamin Selfridge and Peter Selfridge**

Zephyr Press

Chicago

Library of Congress Cataloging-in-Publication Data
Is available from the Library of Congress.

A Kid's Guide to Creating Web Pages for Home and School
Grades 5—10

©2004 by Benjamin Selfridge and Peter Selfridge
Printed in the United States of America
ISBN: 1-56976-180-9
Design and Production: Monica Baziuk
Illustrations: Gary Zamchick
Cover design: Monica Baziuk
Cover photograph: Luc Beziat

FrontPage®, Microsoft® and Windows® are registered trademarks or trademarks of Microsoft
Corporation in the United States and/or other countries. Screen shots reprinted by permission
from Microsoft Corporation.
Google™ is a trademark of Google Inc.
Netscape Navigator® is a registered trademark of Netscape Network.
Opera® is a registered trademark of Opera Software.

Published by:
Zephyr Press
An imprint of Chicago Review Press, Inc.
814 North Franklin Street
Chicago, Illinois 60610
800-232-2187
www.zephyrpress.com

# Contents

## 2. Fun with Fonts
### Creating an Online Journal ⟨13⟩

## 3. Interesting Images
### Creating a Web Photo Album ⟨31⟩

## 7. A Little Bit of JavaScript
### The Power of Programming ⟨85⟩

## 8. Conclusion
### What's Next? ⟨95⟩

# Preface

**MY NAME IS BENJAMIN SELFRIDGE,** and right now (summer 2003) I am thirteen years old. Like most of you, I've been messing around with computers for a long time (well, as long a time as is possible when you're only thirteen). My dad is a computer scientist, so we've pretty much always had a computer at home. My mom and dad bought me various computer games over the years, and I learned how to do word processing and presentations, and use files and folders. I learned how to use the Internet ages ago, and have used it mostly to get information on my hobbies, which have included magic tricks, trading cards, sports, and most recently, video games.

A few years ago (I think when I was ten), a friend told me how to set up a free web page. I forget which site I went to, but it included a bunch of "wizards" that take you through the process one step at a time, without having to do any programming. That was fun, but then I began to get interested in what was really going on. My dad explained a little bit about HTML and showed me how to look at a Web page's underlying HTML using my browser. (This is really great: in Microsoft® Internet Explorer, all you have to do is select "View" and then "Source"—we'll write it like this in the future: View → Source.) He also had a couple of books on HTML, and one day I opened one up and just began to type in the example. Once I realized that if you type in HTML and give the file a name that ends in ".html," it will open up in your browser, I was hooked. I messed around for about six months (so my Dad tells me) and more recently have explored JavaScript (which is really cool), style sheets, and other stuff.

Then one day I had an idea to write a book. Actually, I can't remember if it was my idea or my dad's, but I do remember thinking that it was a really good one. Then, well, you know, we moved on to other things, which is why I'm now thirteen. I'll let my Dad tell you the rest.

**Ben Selfridge**

W ELL, / remember: It was Ben's idea to write this book. I thought it was a great one, and I watched as he learned an amazing amount of material in a short time. This showed me how easy HTML really is and how much fun it can be. I'm a computer scientist by training, so I have a good understanding of computer and Internet technology, but I'm also really interested in kids and education. I thought it would be great if kids could understand the real basis of Web pages and Web browsing by being able to create web

pages directly with HTML. Now, HTML is not computer programming, but it's a step in that direction. (Creating JavaScript programs, on the other hand, is computer programming, and we'll talk a little bit about JavaScript near the end of this book.)

A couple of years went by before I decided to get serious; either the idea was a good one—in which case it was still good—or it wasn't, and why not find out? I discovered several books out there with similar goals, but none written by a kid for kids. It also seemed to me that these other books were too complicated for true beginners. I thought we might be able to make our book different from the others, so I approached some publishers. With the kind attention and help of Ms. Veronica Durie, of Zephyr Press, we made a decision: we were going to go for it! This book is the result, and we hope you enjoy it.

**Peter Selfridge**

*Peter G. Selfridge*

# About This Book

**THERE ARE LOTS OF THINGS** to learn about computers and the Internet, and lots of ways of learning them. Since HTML is the basic technology underlying Web pages, there are plenty of HTML resources out there, including books on HTML for different skill levels, online tutorials for kids, and courses at school, your local community college, and perhaps even your library. So why did we write this book?

DAD, MY SISTER, AND ME

There are a couple of reasons. First, most of the books and other resources seem to us to be too advanced and too complicated for kids. Some are essentially reference books, and others assume the reader is already comfortable with using a computer in a technical way. Second (and this is related to the first reason), we wanted a book for kids. By "kids" we mean other Benjamins, perhaps as young as seven years old, who have grown up with computers, computer games, and the Internet but may never have really explored computer technology. Of course, advanced technology can be mastered only through years of study, but we believe there is no reason why any motivated child or adult cannot learn some straightforward technologies, like HTML.

By the way, since this book is written by both Ben and Ben's dad, we usually use "we" in the text. But sometimes Ben takes over and mentions something from his point of view (usually to his dad's detriment). In those instances, the text switches to "I."

So, how should you use this book? The answer is very easy and reflects our philosophy of learning: sit down at the computer and start at Chapter 1. You'll find that not only do we introduce HTML right away, we also take you through what can be a particularly frustrating aspect of learning computer technology: the actual mechanics of files, folders, and applications. We describe exactly how to set up your environment to facilitate learning the technology, and we take you step-by-step through each new HTML capability. In later chapters, we show you how to integrate HTML capabilities in a Web site and publish it on the Web. Finally, we tease you with some JavaScript and describe some other kinds of technologies you can learn too.

Every chapter ends with a summary and a set of Challenge Questions. We encourage you to answer these questions on your own; some will be quite easy, others a bit more challenging. They are a great way to test yourself and see what you've learned. All the answers are on our Web site: www.html-for-kids.com.

Now, we don't intend this book to be the only one you'll need to become proficient with HTML—far from it! If this book turns you on to HTML, you'll need any number of other, more comprehensive books that can provide the detail you'll need.

# System Requirements

We assume you're using a Microsoft Windows® computer; that is, a computer running Microsoft Windows 98, Microsoft Windows 2000, or Microsoft Windows XP. You're probably using Microsoft Internet Explorer as your Web browser (but that shouldn't matter too much). If you're using a Macintosh, it shouldn't be too hard to follow our approach. The main difference is that the screen shots in this book won't look exactly the same as what you see on your computer.

## Acknowledgments

We'd like to thank a number of people for helping and supporting us in this effort, including Mrs. Susan Cooper, Veronica Durie, Mary Jo Fahey, and members of our family including Caroline, Mallory, Oliver, Allison, Lauren, and Nancy Selfridge.

Finally, and this is our most important and heartfelt message: **HAVE FUN!**

**Peter and Benjamin Selfridge**

# A Kid's Guide to
# CREATING
# WEB PAGES

## for Home and School

# Getting Started
## Your First HTML Page

## Welcome

Everyone probably knows about the World Wide Web, also called the *Internet,* the Web, and even, in the "old days" (1995 or so) the Information Superhighway (which sounds pretty lame, even to my dad). My friends and I just call it the Internet, as in "Did you get that off the Internet?" and we, like you, have grown up with it. The Internet is a humongous communications network of linked computers all around

the world. Once you log on to the Internet, you can access a virtually unlimited amount of information from any of the computers on the network.

Everybody we know uses the Internet to *browse* (that is, go to different Web sites) for information for homework, hobbies, and games. I've used it to find out about magic tricks, get trading card information and cheat codes for video games, view cool animations, check local movie times, play interactive games, and chat with other kids located all over the world. My Dad uses it to get news (boring—well, usually); check the stock market; buy stuff from online companies; find out about animals, nature, and hiking (my Dad's a real outdoors nut); and do his work as a computer scientist.

You should be familiar with the terms *Web page* and *browsing,* since that's how you use the Internet. As you know, a *Web site* is a collection of Web pages hosted by a person, business, or organization. Each different screen you open on the Web site is a *Web page.* Browsing is how you get from one Web site to another, by typing in a URL (address) or clicking on a link. (We'll talk more about links in Chapter 5.)

Probably some of you have heard of HTML, and maybe you even know that that's how Web pages are created. Some of you have probably even created your own Web pages using Web site "wizards" and tools such as Microsoft FrontPage® computer software. These ways of creating Web pages are fairly easy—all you have to do is to enter the information you want on your page as prompted, make the selections you want, and voilà! You have a Web page. But there is a downside: not only is it not quite as easy as it seems at first, but you don't learn what's actually going on. This is a problem, as far as we're concerned.

This book is about how to create Web pages by writing HTML directly. *HTML* stands for "hypertext markup language," and my Dad tells me that *hypertext* means text with links in it, like the buttons on Web pages that send you from one page to another. But that doesn't matter. What does matter is that writing HTML is really easy and really fun, and it allows you to make your Web page look exactly the way you want it to. The other cool thing about writing HTML is that it's just the beginning of learning other nifty stuff like JavaScript, XML, and Java. My dad has helped me do a little bit of stuff like this, and it's really fun. I'll be showing you a little JavaScript near the end of this book.

OK, let's get started!

# Setting Up the Basics

The first thing you need to do is to create a folder for your work. We suggest you put it on the *desktop,* the main computer screen. You probably know how to do this, but in case you don't, it's easy. Just right-click (click the right mouse button and hold it down), and a little menu will appear. Scroll down to "New," then over to "Folder." When you click on "Folder," a folder named "New Folder" will appear. You can rename the folder anything you want to call it by right-clicking on the folder and scrolling down to "Rename." Now, the name of the folder is highlighted, and you can change it by typing in a new name (and moving the cursor with the mouse or arrow keys if you like). Note: "Rename" is right under "Delete," which can cause a problem if you're not careful. Figure 1.1 shows what this looks like on our computer, with a new folder already created and renamed "My HTML."

OK, now you've got your folder with some clever name like "My HTML." Now let's put into your folder some shortcuts to the two tools you will be using most often: Microsoft Notepad and your browser. A *shortcut* is just a link that you

Figure 1.1. A Windows desktop, showing the menus you use to create a new folder. You can see a new "My HTML" folder in the upper left. (You can put your folder anywhere on the desktop you like.)

click on to open a file or program. Your *browser* is what you use to get around the Internet. With a Windows computer, your browser is probably Internet Explorer, but you could use a different browser like Netscape Navigator or Opera.

Assuming your new folder and the browser icon (picture) are both on the desktop, you can right-click on the browser icon, drag it to the folder, release, and choose "Create Shortcut(s) Here." Do the same thing with Notepad, which you should be able to find under Start → Programs → Accessories. (This means to click on the "Start" button in the lower right, scroll to "Programs," and scroll to "Accessories." You probably know this already.) Now your folder should look something like Figure 1.2 when you open it (double-click, or right-click and select "Open").

Figure 1.2. Open "My HTML" folder with shortcuts to Notepad and the Internet Explorer Web browser.

## Creating a Basic HTML Page

OK, now you're ready to create your first HTML page. There are two parts to this process. First you need to create the HTML file that describes your page, and second you need to make it come up in your browser. Making the page appear in your browser is easy if you name the file properly. But first things first.

Open up Notepad by double-clicking on the shortcut you just made. Then type in the following:

```
<html>
<head>
<title>Hello World</title>
</head>
<body>
Hello, World!
</body>
</html>
```

And, yes, we will tell you what all this means throughout this chapter.

The first thing to learn is that almost everything you just typed is a tag. A *tag* is a piece of text surrounded by angle brackets (< >). It is an HTML command that tells your browser what to do. The second thing to learn is that most tags come in pairs, with the second tag being the same as the first except for a slash like this: /. You can think of the / as meaning "stop". So, if one tag says <html>, a bit later you'll see an </html> tag. One way to think about this is the first tag means "start the HTML section of the Web page" and the second means "stop the HTML section of the Web page." Tags are important for organization and to keep the meaning clear. (It's also important to get into the habit of using these tags, and this book will teach you that.)

### ⓘ TRY THIS!

By the way, the background of the desktop is really easy to change. Here's how: If you right-click your mouse on the background and scroll down to "Properties," you'll get a "Display Properties" menu. There's a bunch of stuff here, but there should be a tab for "Background." It will allow you to choose from a set of background images, preview each one, and choose whatever picture you want for your background. Try it!

You can even use a picture you get off the Internet, or from a scanner or digital camera, for your desktop background. Can you see how?

Every HTML program has to be surrounded by the `<html>` and `</html>` tags. This is what indicates to your browser that you are using HTML.

Next, there is a `<head>` section and within the head a title. ("Head" stands for heading, and why they don't just let you type "heading," we don't know.) The `<title>` tag just gives your Web page a title. (Really? Amazing, isn't it?) Whatever is between the `<title>` tags shows up on the little colored strip (sometimes called the *title bar*) that you see at the very top of your browser window. Since you typed "Hello World" between the `<title>` and `</title>` tags, "Hello World" will show up at the top of your window.

Finally, there's the body. Under the `<body>` tag is where you put all the stuff that will appear on your Web page. This is a good time to bring to mind the real purpose of a Web page: it's to provide or present or display information. Because the most basic kind of information on the Web is text, a basic Web page consists of some text. In the example, we've put just two words: "Hello, World!" If you like, you can type any words you choose here and you'll see them displayed on your Web page.

# Displaying Your Page

OK, now that you understand what you typed into Notepad, how do you get the browser to recognize the HTML and do what you've told it to do? It's pretty easy: all you have to do is to save the file with the proper kind of name. This takes a couple of steps. First, select "Save As" from the "File" menu of your open Notepad document, and the form shown in Figure 1.3 pops up (this is called a *dialog box*).

At the top of the dialog box you'll see "Save in:" and a small box. You have to make sure the folder you created in the first part of this chapter shows in this box. Select the little downward arrow tab on the right and you'll get a list of folders on your desktop. Figure 1.4 shows the folders on our desktop, with the "My HTML" folder we created for our Web pages.

**Figure 1.3.** "Save As" dialog box in Notepad.

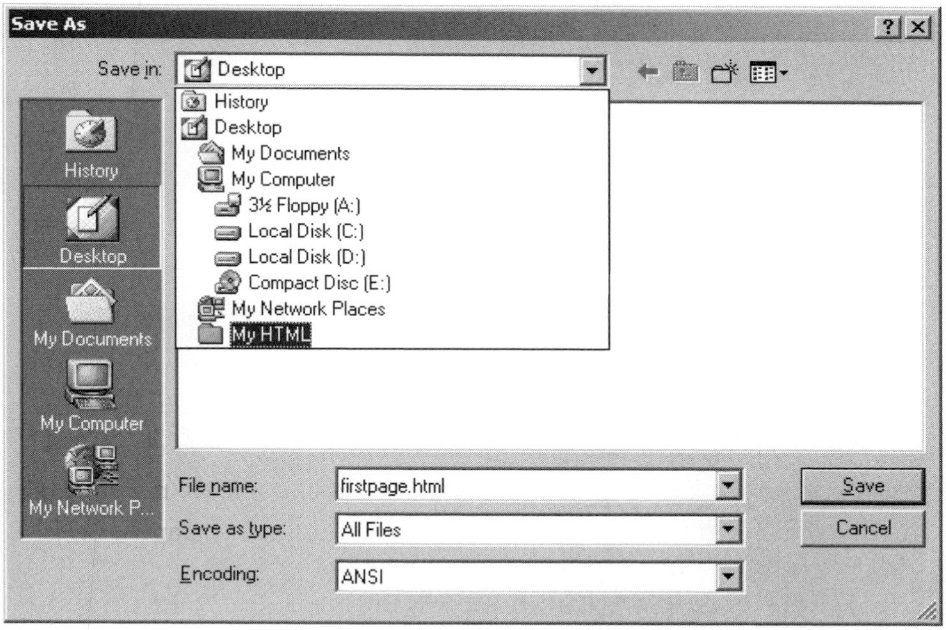

**Figure 1.4.** Choosing the right folder to save your Web page in. Note that the "Save as type" box at the bottom of the window has been set to "All Files."

Scroll down to "My HTML," or whatever you called your folder. (It should be indented under "Desktop" because it's on the desktop.) Click once and the file name should show up in the "Save in" box. You're all set with this part.

Now you need to save your file with a name ending with the file extension ".html." (A *file extension* is three or four letters after a . at the end of the file name.) To do this, you have to change the "Save as type" box to "All Files" (as we've done in Figure 1.4). (Again, click on the downward arrow and select the "All Files" choice.) Then, in the "File name" box, type "firstpage.html" and hit the "Save" button. Your file will be written into your HTML folder and will magically have the browser icon, which is the icon for HTML files (see Figure 1.5).

Figure 1.5. Open "My HTML" folder containing the saved "firstpage" file.

Now, if you double-click on the "firstpage" file, your web browser will start right up and show you what's in the file, like you see in Figure 1.6.

**ⓘ DID YOU KNOW?**

Every piece of information in your computer is stored in a file. Even a folder is a file. Files typically have a name and an extension. The extension is the three or four letters after the . at the end of the file name. For example, in the file called "historypaper.doc," the *file name* is "historypaper" and the *extension* is "doc." The extension determines what application the computer will use to open a file. You probably know that Microsoft Word opens ".doc" files, Notepad opens ".txt" files, and your browser opens ".html" files.

**Hello World - Microsoft Internet Explorer**

File  Edit  View  Favorites  Tools  Help

← Back  →  ⊗ ⬢ ⌂  Search  Favorites  History  

Address  C:\Documents and Settings\Administrator\Desktop\My HTML\firstpage.html  Go  Links »

Hello, World!

Done      My Computer

**Figure 1.6.** Open "firstpage" file showing the Web page you created.

Congratulations! You've created your first Web page. Before you start celebrating, though, try two more things. First, see the title at the top of the page where it says "Hello World - Microsoft Internet Explorer"? Let's change that to a different title. Second, let's put more text in the body of the Web page, so you can see how the text starts wrapping.

To make these changes, you will have to open your "firstpage" file in Notepad again. But wait a minute! Since you renamed your file "firstpage.html," it now appears with a browser icon. If you just double-click on the file, it will open in your browser. So how do you open it using Notepad instead? Put your cursor on the file and, once again, you can use the good old right-click method. But this time select "Open With," then "Choose Program." This will bring up the window you see in Figure 1.7.

Scroll down until you see Notepad (as shown) and click on it. *Do not* check the "Always use this program to open these files" checkbox at the

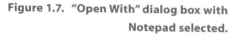

**Open With**   ? ✕

Click the program you want to use to open 'firstpage.html'.
If the program is not in the list, click Other.

Choose the program you want to use:

- Microsoft Access for Windows
- Microsoft Excel for Windows
- Microsoft FrontPage
- Microsoft Paint
- Microsoft PowerPoint for Windows
- Microsoft Word for Windows
- Notepad

☐ Always use this program to open these files

OK    Cancel    Other...

**Figure 1.7.** "Open With" dialog box with Notepad selected.

bottom of the dialog box. Now, every time you need to edit the file, right-click on it. Notepad should be available under the "Open With" menu item.

So start up Notepad again and change what follows the **<title>** tag to "This is my first Web page," so that this phrase will appear in the title bar. Second, still in Notepad, type something a bit longer than "Hello, World!" in the body section. For example, "Benjamin and Peter Selfridge have written an awesome book, and I hope they sell a gazillion copies and make tons of money and the dad (Peter) should absolutely give the son (Ben) at least half of it so he can buy lots of video games and other books on cool technologies, and I guess putting some of it into a college fund is a good idea." You'll see that the text wraps from the first line onto the next lines. If you change the size of your browser window, you'll see that the text wrapping changes automatically. We're going to use this characteristic in the next chapter.

## Summary

In this chapter, we've covered how to set up your computer desktop with a folder to hold all your work and shortcuts to the two main tools you'll use, Notepad and your browser. Then, we showed you how to create your first Web page by typing in a few lines of HTML primarily as tags, which are HTML commands. Finally, we showed you how to display the Web page in your browser by renaming it with the ".html" file extension. You're off and running!

# Challenge Questions 🔍

**1** Take your first Web page file ("firstpage.html") and copy it and rename it. (How about "page2.html"?) Now open the copy using Notepad and type in a couple of sentences separated by a couple of blank lines. Then display the file using your browser. What happens?

**2** Change the text between the `<title>` and `</title>` tags to anything you want. What happens when you display the page in your browser?

**3** Now remove the `</title>` tag and display the page again. What happens? Why?

**4** Right-click on your desktop and change the background.

You can find the solutions to these challenge questions on our Web site: www.html-for-kids.com.

# Fun with Fonts

## Creating an Online Journal

## Creating a Personal Journal

Why in the world would anyone want to create a journal on the Web? Well, by "personal journal" we don't necessarily mean a diary with all your biggest secrets in it. We just mean a bunch of information that you'd like to put in one place, like a report. So, we're going to pretend that you participate in base-

### THIS CHAPTER WILL

→ explain how to do your work with Notepad and your browser open side-by-side, which makes Web page creation easier;

→ show you how to add spaces and paragraphs to your work to improve its appearance;

→ introduce heading tags that help you organize your Web page;

→ show you how to change the color and style of your fonts and play with the spacing of your text to create an attractive Web page;

→ show you how to put it all together to create an online journal.

ball and you've been assigned to write a report on each game. Sound good? (Of course, who knows, maybe you really *are* a baseball nut.)

The first thing to do is to create a new file for your journal. The easiest (and thus almost always the best) way to do this is just to copy and rename an HTML file you've already created, such as your "firstpage.html" file. To do this, open up the folder that you created in the last chapter, position the mouse over the "firstpage" icon, hold down the right mouse button, and drag

**Figure 2.1. Making a copy of a file by dragging the icon.**

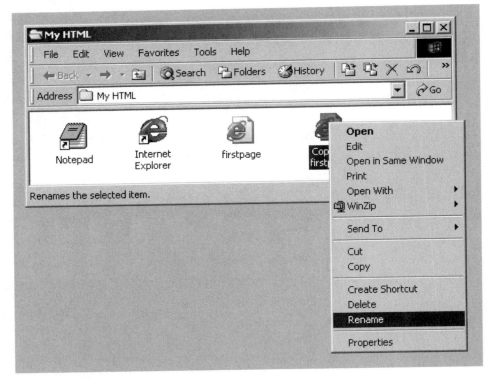

**Figure 2.2. Renaming the copied file.**

it over to an empty part of the folder. When you release the button, a menu will pop up that looks like the one in Figure 2.1.

The menu gives you a choice to "Copy," "Move," or "Create a Shortcut." You want to select "Copy." You'll get a new file and icon (the little picture that stands for the file) that says "Copy of firstpage." Now you can rename the new

```
myjournal1 - Notepad
File  Edit  Format  Help
<html>
<head>
<title>Hello World</title>
</head>
<body>
Sports Journal for the Warren Wildcats

by Ben Selfridge

Coach:  Sam Johnston
Assistant Coaches:        Susan Griffin
                          Peter Selfridge
                          Thomas Kirk

Team members:     Ben Selfridge
                  Tom Chagall
                  Fred Murskinski
                  Bob Barlett
                  Kelly Mi
                  Michael Jennings
                  Eric Kestler
                  Arthur Stevens
                  Brayden Kirk
                  Lohn Graden
                  Loren Terveen

Game 1

September 5, 2003

Opponent: Green Brook Dragons

The Wildcats were the home team at Muir Field, so the Dragons
started on a fine Saturday afternoon, sunny and not too hot. Mrs.
Selfridge was kind enough to bring Gatorade for the entire
team, so we didn't get dehydrated. Loren Terveen pitched the first
5 innings. The Dragons put two men on base but didn't score, and the
Wildcats went down 1, 2, 3. Not a good beginning. The Dragons then
scored 2 runs on a single, a walk, a single that filled the bases,
and, after two men out, a single that drove 2 runs home. Terveen
got that last man out. Two innings went by with no more runs. Finally,
Kelly Mi was walked and Ben Selfridge's single drove him to
third. Brayden Kirk hit a solid hit to center field, and Mi came home.
Ben was on third. Kestler struck out (the Dragons' pitching was
excellent the entire game), but Stevens got a single and Selfridge
came home to tie up the game. The next two innings were not as
exciting, but both teams scored a single run. Then, in the final
inning, the Dragon's main pitcher was replaced and the Wildcats
went wild! 4 runs later, the final score was:

Wildcats: 7     Dragons: 3

</body>
</html>
```

**Figure 2.3. Sample text for a journal created in Notepad.**

file by right-clicking (you know what this means by now) over it so that the pull-down menu appears as shown in Figure 2.2.

Select "Rename" (down near the bottom); the menu will disappear and the cursor will be positioned inside the text under the file icon. Now you can type in a new name for your file. Rename your file "myjournal1." (By the way, since you did this in the first chapter and again here, from now on we'll assume that you know how to copy and rename files.)

After you've created the copy, open it using Notepad as we described on page 9 in Chapter 1 (remember, right-click and select "Open With" then "Notepad"). Now leave all the HTML tags in place, just deleting the text between the tags. Type in an account of your baseball team, maybe something like the one in Figure 2.3, and then save the file.

But, now, here's a problem: When you double-click on the icon to bring up the file in your browser, the result is what you see in Figure 2.4.

Hmm. That wasn't quite what we had in mind. There must be some kind of solution.

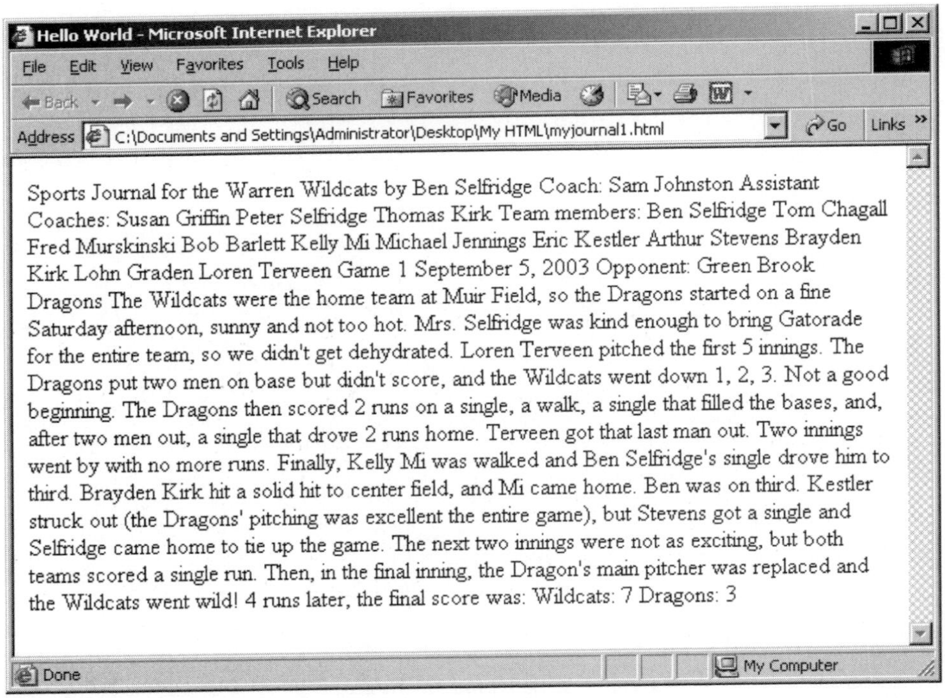

Figure 2.4. How the journal in Figure 2.3 looks in your browser.

Sports Journal for the Warren Wildcats by Ben Selfridge Coach: Sam Johnston Assistant Coaches: Susan Griffin Peter Selfridge Thomas Kirk Team members: Ben Selfridge Tom Chagall Fred Murskinski Bob Barlett Kelly Mi Michael Jennings Eric Kestler Arthur Stevens Brayden Kirk Lohn Graden Loren Terveen Game 1 September 5, 2003 Opponent: Green Brook Dragons The Wildcats were the home team at Muir Field, so the Dragons started on a fine Saturday afternoon, sunny and not too hot. Mrs. Selfridge was kind enough to bring Gatorade for the entire team, so we didn't get dehydrated. Loren Terveen pitched the first 5 innings. The Dragons put two men on base but didn't score, and the Wildcats went down 1, 2, 3. Not a good beginning. The Dragons then scored 2 runs on a single, a walk, a single that filled the bases, and, after two men out, a single that drove 2 runs home. Terveen got that last man out. Two innings went by with no more runs. Finally, Kelly Mi was walked and Ben Selfridge's single drove him to third. Brayden Kirk hit a solid hit to center field, and Mi came home. Ben was on third. Kestler struck out (the Dragons' pitching was excellent the entire game), but Stevens got a single and Selfridge came home to tie up the game. The next two innings were not as exciting, but both teams scored a single run. Then, in the final inning, the Dragon's main pitcher was replaced and the Wildcats went wild! 4 runs later, the final score was: Wildcats: 7 Dragons: 3

# Making Breaks and Paragraphs

Aha! The answer is breaks and paragraphs.

A *break* (making the text start on a new line) is done using the break tag `<br>`, and a *paragraph,* which is really a break then a blank line, is `<p>`. Neither of these tags has an ending tag; that is, you don't need to use `</p>` or `</br>`. (However, in future versions of HTML, the `</p>` tag may be required. Don't forget that HTML is always evolving.)

We still need to figure out what both of these tags do exactly, and how to add them so that they will help our journal look better. (Our main goal in this book is to help you understand what's going on, instead of just having you copy down a bunch of stuff. Copying is easy. Understanding is much more powerful . . . and more fun!)

First, put `<br>`s in your "myjournal1" file wherever you want to start a new line. Here's the top part of the file as an example:

```
<html>
<head>
<title>Hello World</title>
</head>
<body>
Sports Journal for the Warren Wildcats
<br>
by Ben Selfridge
<br>
Coach: Sam Johnston
Assistant Coaches:      Susan Griffin
                        Peter Selfridge
                        Thomas Kirk

<br>
Team members:           Ben Selfridge
                        Tom Chagall
```

Figure 2.5 shows what you get in your browser if you do that in the appropriate places.

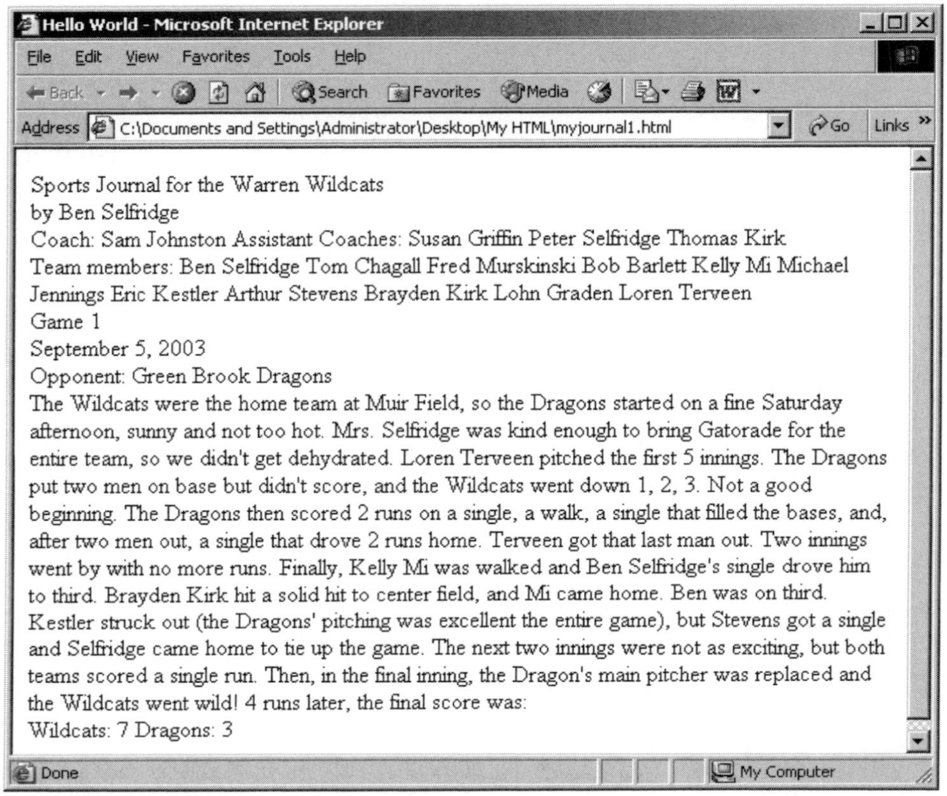

**Figure 2.5. How the journal text looks in your browser with breaks (<br>) inserted.**

While this is clearly an improvement, it's still not quite what we want. Before we fix it, let's make sure we understand what we did. The break tag (**<br>**) makes the text after it start on a new line. This is the first step toward properly formatting our journal (that is, making it look good).

**Figure 2.6. Replacing the break tags (<br>) with paragraph tags (<p>).**

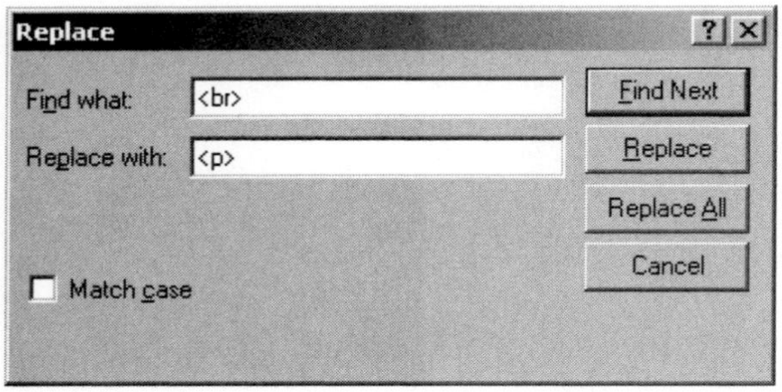

Now try replacing all the **<br>**s with **<p>**s, to see what happens; a really easy way to do this in Notepad is to select Edit → Replace, and you'll get this form to fill out (we've filled it out in Figure 2.6).

Then click "Replace All" and you're all set. Notepad will go through your entire file and replace every occurrence of **<br>** with **<p>**, changing all of your break tags into paragraph tags. Now your Web page will look like you see in Figure 2.7 when you open it in your browser.

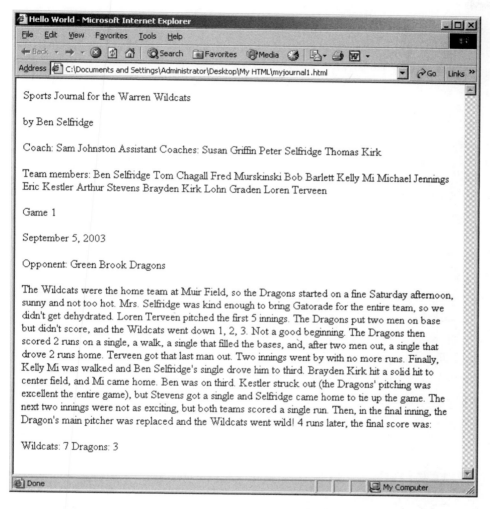

Figure 2.7. How the journal text looks in your browser with paragraphs (`<p>`) inserted.

This looks much better, but we want to make two things clear. First, just because we replaced all the `<br>` tags with `<p>` tags doesn't mean that the `<br>` tag is useless. There are lots of times when you want a break without making a new paragraph—you'll see some examples later in the book. Second, before you do a global search and replace (that is, you replace all occurrences of one word or tag with another), you'd better be sure that this is really what you want to do. You can easily mess up your file in ways that are hard to fix. ("Undo" under the Edit menu in Notepad will undo a change if you realize

You may have figured this out already, but HTML ignores so-called white space—including spaces, tabs, and even hard returns (the Enter key). This can be a bit confusing at first. It means, for example, that it doesn't make any difference whether tags are on their own line or not:

⟨h1⟩This is a heading⟨/h1⟩
or ⟨h1⟩
This is a heading ⟨/h1⟩

Either way, the text looks exactly the same.

you made a mistake right away.) But in this case, there are no examples of "⟨br⟩" that you want to keep, so you're OK.

I'll bet you can figure out all by yourself how to use the ⟨br⟩ tag to make the coaches' and players' names appear in a list rather than run together, which will make the page look even better. (See? We told you ⟨br⟩ can be useful.) That leaves two other things to do: (1) Play with the size and style of the fonts (the style of the type), which we're about to do; and (2) indent lines, which we'll cover later.

# Working with Notepad and Your Browser at the Same Time

Before we go on, we're going to show you a really cool way to learn HTML faster: keep the Notepad file and the browser open at the same time. That is, open the Notepad file by right-clicking on the "myjournal1" icon and choosing Open With ➜ Notepad. You should get the file you typed in. Then, double-click the icon (which is the same as opening it using your browser), and you'll get the Web page. Now, you can change the Notepad file, save the results using File ➜ Save or Ctrl+S, then hit the "Refresh" button on the browser.

Voilà! The browser shows the new Web page. This allows you to go back and forth, making changes in your Notepad file, saving then, then checking the result right away in the browser. This is a much more efficient way to work than opening only one application at a time.

Figure 2.8 is a shot of a screen that shows this.

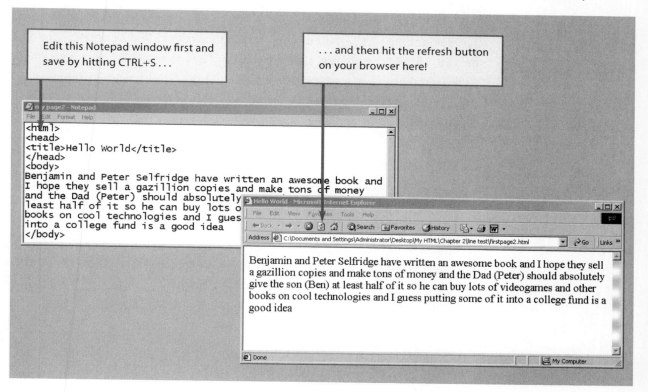

## Changing Font Size Using the Heading Tag

Do you know what a font is? If you've used word processing software, you probably do: a *font* is basically a certain kind of lettering, or technically a typeface, and there are hundreds if not thousands of them. Leaving the type of font alone, let's change the font size in the easiest way possible: with heading tags.

Heading tags are easy. There are six of them, with matching end tags, and they look like this:

```
<h1>  </h1>        <h4>  </h4>
<h2>  </h2>        <h5>  </h5>
<h3>  </h3>        <h6>  </h6>
```

You get the idea. A pair of heading tags makes the text between them bigger. So, `<h1>` is the biggest size of heading, `<h2>` the next biggest, and so on. To try out these tags, edit your "myjournal1" file and put heading tags around the text that you want to make larger. We'd suggest using heading 1 (`<h1>`) for the title, heading 2 for the author, heading 3 for the "coach" and "team members" lines, and heading 2 for the line that says "Game 1." Here's how your tags will look in Notepad:

```
<html>
<head>
<title>My journal</title>
</head>
<body>
<h1>Sports Journal for the Warren Wildcats</h2>
<p>
<h2>by Ben Selfridge</h2>
<p>
<h3>Coach: Sam Johnston</h3>
<p>
<h3>Assistant Coaches:</h3>
<br>
Susan Griffin
<br>
Peter Selfridge
<br>
```

```
Thomas Kirk
<p>
```

Note that we've put in the **<br>** tags to separate the names, as we talked about earlier. Now, your Web page looks much, much better (see Figure 2.9)!

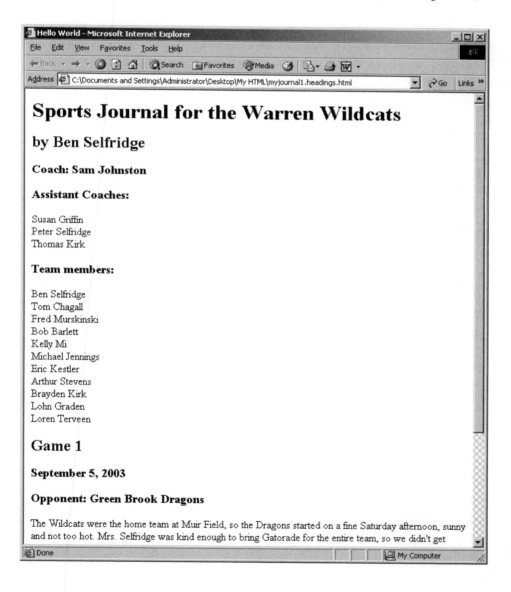

# Spicing Up Text: The Direct Method

At this point, our journal is looking pretty good. But the actual text describing the game is starting to look a little tame, now that we've added headings of different sizes. Let's look at three other ways of changing the appearance of the text. (If you've used Microsoft Word, you're probably familiar with all three.) These are making text bold, italic, or underlined. And, yes, you can combine these. Let's take a look. Each type style has its own pair of tags, a beginning tag that goes in front of the text you want to change the appearance of, and an end tag that turns off the effect. These tags are particularly easy to remember:

| | | |
|---|---|---|
| Bold: | `<b>` | `</b>` |
| Italic: | `<i>` | `</i>` |
| Underline: | `<u>` | `</u>` |

Let's make a really simple example. (From now on, we'll usually skip putting in the basic `<html>`, `<body>`, and other "boilerplate," or standard, tags in our examples. We assume you know how to put them in by now. So here's some HTML:

```
<h3><u>Text Spice:</u></h3>
Here is some text that is <b>bold</b>, <i>italic</i>, and
<u>underlined</u>. And here's some text that is formatted
using <b><i><u>all three tags!!!!</b>
</i></u>. Cool, huh?
```

Notice that we underlined the heading, to show you that you really can combine these tags with any other text tags. Just remember to think about a tag as meaning start, like this: `<i>` means "start italics," and you'll have an easier time remembering to include `</i>` for "end italics."

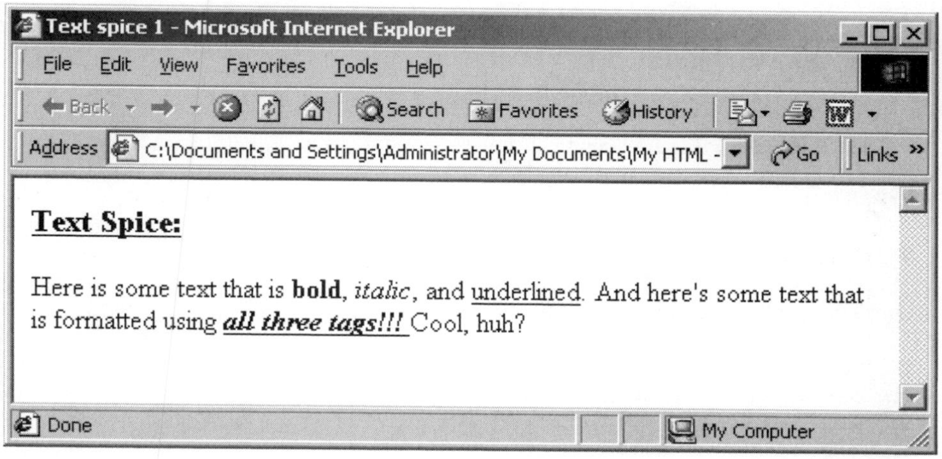

Text spice 1 - Microsoft Internet Explorer
File Edit View Favorites Tools Help
Back Search Favorites History
Address C:\Documents and Settings\Administrator\My Documents\My HTML -
Go Links
Text Spice:
Here is some text that is bold, italic, and underlined. And here's some text that is formatted using all three tags!!! Cool, huh?
Done
My Computer


**Figure 2.10. Examples of bold, italic, and underlined text, and all three together.**

# Spicing Up Text: The Indirect Method

There's another way of spicing up text that we'll call the indirect method. We'll show you two ways of doing this: the emphasis tag and the strong tag. Both of these need the usual end tags. Here's how each one looks in Notepad:

```
I want to <em>emphasize</em> the word "emphasize."
I want the word "strong" to look <strong>strong</strong>.
```

Now, if you go to the description of the game and surround every player's name with the emphasis tag, here's what the game description will look like (see Figure 2.11).

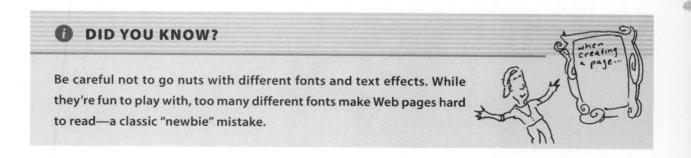

**DID YOU KNOW?**

**Be careful not to go nuts with different fonts and text effects. While they're fun to play with, too many different fonts make Web pages hard to read—a classic "newbie" mistake.**

when creating a page...

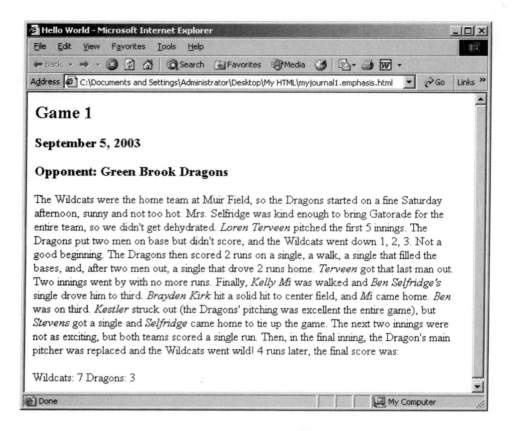

If you replace the emphasis tag with the strong tag (remembering to change the end tags too!), you get Figure 2.12, which we think looks even better. (Can you remember how to do a global replace? See page 18.)

And that looks pretty good!

# Fonts and the Font Tag

As the last example shows, there are often different ways of accomplishing the same thing in HTML, and we're going to see another example here. You've already learned how to make text larger using heading tags, but those tags don't let you enlarge just a few words inside a paragraph. You can do that using the font tag: **<font>**. As you'll see, you can add a number of attributes to this tag, including one to change the typeface and the color of the text.

> **Hello World - Microsoft Internet Explorer**
>
> File   Edit   View   Favorites   Tools   Help
>
> ← Back  →  ⊗ ⊠ ⌂  ⊗Search  ⊠Favorites  ⊗Media  ⊗  ⊠▾ ⊜ ⊠ ▾
>
> Address  C:\Documents and Settings\Administrator\Desktop\My HTML\myjournal1.strong.html   ▾  ⊘Go  Links »
>
> # Game 1
>
> ### September 5, 2003
>
> ### Opponent: Green Brook Dragons
>
> The Wildcats were the home team at Muir Field, so the Dragons started on a fine Saturday afternoon, sunny and not too hot. Mrs. Selfridge was kind enough to bring Gatorade for the entire team, so we didn't get dehydrated. **Loren Terveen** pitched the first 5 innings. The Dragons put two men on base but didn't score, and the Wildcats went down 1, 2, 3. Not a good beginning. The Dragons then scored 2 runs on a single, a walk, a single that filled the bases, and, after two men out, a single that drove 2 runs home. **Terveen** got that last man out. Two innings went by with no more runs. Finally, **Kelly Mi** was walked and **Ben Selfridge's** single drove him to third. **Brayden Kirk** hit a solid hit to center field, and **Mi** came home. **Ben** was on third. **Kestler** struck out (the Dragons' pitching was excellent the entire game), but **Stevens** got a single and **Selfridge** came home to tie up the game. The next two innings were not as exciting, but both teams scored a single run. Then, in the final inning, the Dragon's main pitcher was replaced and the Wildcats went wild! 4 runs later, the final score was:
>
> Wildcats: 7 Dragons: 3
>
> Done     My Computer

*Attributes* are just additional characteristics that go inside the tag. Here's a simple example:

```
<html>
<head>
<title>Font1</title>
</head>
<body>
Once upon a time there lived a small <font face="Impact"
   size=5 color=purple> squirrel</font> named Ziggy.
</body>
</html>
```

### TRY THIS

**To find out what fonts are available (at least on Internet Explorer), use the Tools menu and select "Internet Options." At the bottom of the "General" tab you'll see a button labeled "Fonts." Be sure to use these names in quotes inside a <font> tag, as we've shown you.**

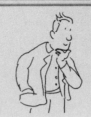

The font tag allows you to set the color of the type, the size, and the typeface. Here, we specify the typeface called Impact. The attributes are pretty straightforward, but it does help to know that there are seven sizes of fonts (**size=1**, **size=2**, and so on). Colors can be represented either by name (there are a bunch of names, including the standard colors such as red, green, blue, and so on) or by hexadecimal code (**#rrggbb**). (Don't ask what hexadecimals are; it doesn't really matter.) You can use these to create any color combination of red, green, and blue that you want.

Figure 2.13 shows what the preceding HTML looks like in your browser (minus the color, which doesn't show up in this book). When you do this exercise yourself, you'll see the color on your screen.

Font1 - Microsoft Internet Explorer
File Edit View Favorites Tools Help
Back Search Favorites History
Address C:\Documents and Settings\Administrator\Desktop\My HTML
Go
Links
Once upon a time there lived a small squirrel named Ziggy.
Done
My Computer

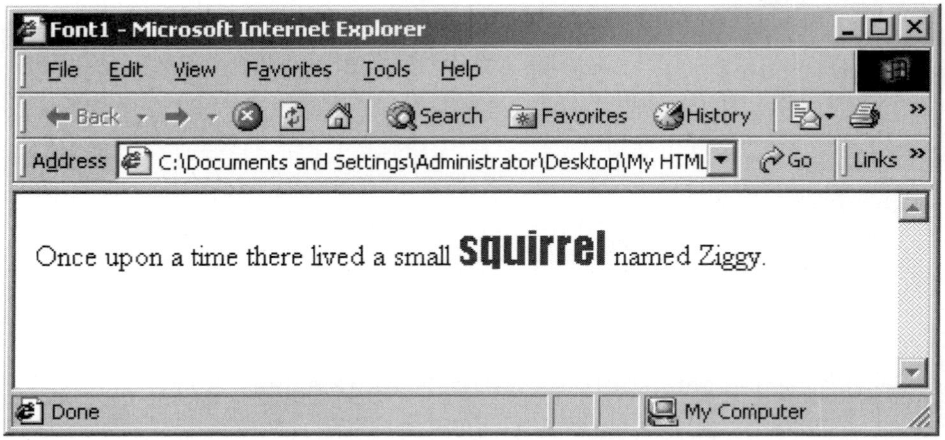

**Figure 2.13. Changing the appearance of a word using the font tag and attributes.**

# Positioning Text on the Page

You can use lots of other tags to make your text look the way you want it to. We're not going to go over all of them, but here are some tags for positioning text on your page. Figure 2.14 shows what each one looks like on a Web page.

```
<html>
<head>
<title>Hello World</title>
</head>
<body>
<center><h1>This is centered on the page!</h1></center>
<p align=right>This text is aligned to the right!
<p align=left>This text is aligned to the left!
<p align=center>This is another way to center text!
</body>
</html>
```

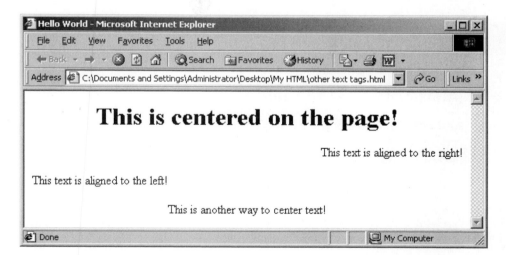

Figure 2.14. Centered and aligned text.

# Summary

Wow, you have made really great progress. You've learned how to create and nicely format an online journal using breaks and paragraphs, headings, and bold, italic, and underlined text. You also got a brief introduction to the **<font>** tag, which allows you change the typeface of a word, and you know how to center text or align it with the left or right edge of the screen. You also saw a really convenient way to work with Notepad and your browser open side-by-side.

# Challenge Questions 🔍

**1** What is the difference between the break tag **<br>** and the paragraph tag **<p>**?

**2** Take the journal file as we had it in Figure 2.5 and add breaks to separate the names of the coaches and assistant coaches.

**3** Create a page that uses all six heading tags so that the text "This is heading 1" appears in heading 1, the text "This is heading 2" appears in heading 2, and so on.

**4** Leave out an **</h>** tag. What happens?

**5** Add bold to heading 3. What happens? Why?

# Interesting Images

## Creating a Web Photo Album

## Images and Image Files

We think you'll agree that in the last chapter, things began to get interesting. Breaking the text into sections, adding heading tags, and using italics and bold for emphasis resulted in a really nice-looking Web page. However, the Web is about much more than just text, and putting images on your Web page is the first step toward multimedia Web content. (*Multimedia* means images, sounds, and even movie clips!)

First it's worthwhile to understand what a digital image really is. It's really just a big array of numbers, where each number represents the amount of color in a *pixel,* or picture element. Let's look at an example. To keep things simple at first, imagine a black-and-white image of black stripes on a white background with dimensions of 100 by 100 pixels (100 pixels wide by 100 pixels high). The stripes in our image will be 5 pixels wide and separated by 5 pixels. Figure 3.1 shows the image and then, blown up, the array of numbers that corresponds to part of it. Note that 0 means "no color," that is, black, and 255 means "all color," that is, white.

**Figure 3.1.  A simple image of black-and-white stripes, showing the pixels that make up the pattern.**

```
255 255 255 255 255  0  0  0  0  0  255 255 255 255 255
255 255 255 255 255  0  0  0  0  0  255 255 255 255 255
255 255 255 255 255  0  0  0  0  0  255 255 255 255 255
255 255 255 255 255  0  0  0  0  0  255 255 255 255 255
255 255 255 255 255  0  0  0  0  0  255 255 255 255 255
255 255 255 255 255  0  0  0  0  0  255 255 255 255 255
255 255 255 255 255  0  0  0  0  0  255 255 255 255 255
255 255 255 255 255  0  0  0  0  0  255 255 255 255 255
255 255 255 255 255  0  0  0  0  0  255 255 255 255 255
255 255 255 255 255  0  0  0  0  0  255 255 255 255 255
255 255 255 255 255  0  0  0  0  0  255 255 255 255 255
255 255 255 255 255  0  0  0  0  0  255 255 255 255 255
255 255 255 255 255  0  0  0  0  0  255 255 255 255 255
```

What about color images? Well, every pixel is represented by three numbers, one for the red value, one for the blue value, and one for the green value. So a pixel with the color purple would be represented by the numbers 255, 255, 0, that is, all red, all blue, and no green.

Images are stored on your computer as files, just like any other kind of data. There are many different kinds of image *formats,* or ways of storing images, which are indicated by the file extension, as discussed in Chapter 1. The most common formats are *bitmap,* stored with the extension .bmp, *GIF,* stored with the extension .gif, and *JPEG,* stored with the extension .jpg. Typically, Web images are either .gif or .jpg (GIF or JPEG format). Many applications will allow you to save images in different formats, but this isn't really important right now.

Where can you get images? Two possible sources are a scanner or a digital camera. We're not going to talk about these, because the end result is the same: you have an image file that you can put on your Web page. Another way to create an image is to use a drawing program like Microsoft Paint, which comes with every Windows PC (at least as far as we know). You can usually find it under Start → Programs → Accessories → Paint. If you create an image using Paint, you should save it using GIF or JPEG formats, not bitmap. The file will be much smaller that way, which is especially important if you plan on using the image in a Web page.

The easiest way to get an image is to take it from the Web itself. But be careful how you use images from the Web because many of them are copyrighted. This means that someone owns the image, and you can't use it without that person's permission. Look for images that are in "public domain"; that means anyone is free to use them. To save an image from the Web, all you have to do is to right-click on it, then select "Save Picture As." Be sure to save the image as whatever type shows up in the dialogue box. We suggest you save all your images in a separate folder within your HTML folder. For this book, call the new folder "images."

# Using the Basic Image Tag to Put an Image on a Web Page

Now that you know a little about images and image files, let's take the first step toward putting an image on a Web page. Let's first use familiar tags to create a new page with a title and a heading. As always, we'll put in some extras (underlining and italics) that you've already learned.

```
<html>
<head>
<title>My dad in the morning</title>
</head>
```

```
<body>
<h1 align = center><b><i>Hey!!! Look at my dad when he
  first wakes up in the morning!!!</b></i></h1>
</body>
</html>
```

Call this file image1.html. This results in a page like the one you see in Figure 3.2.

Figure 3.2. Heading for
image1 file.

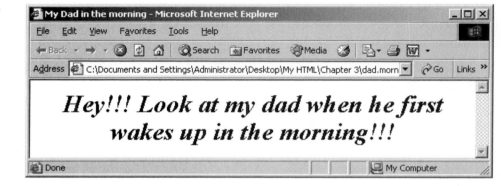

Now let's add an image tag in the simplest possible form. We're going to add an image file called "sillydad.gif," which is in the "images" folder within the "My HTML" folder.

```
<html>
<head>
<title>My dad in the morning</title>
</head>
<body>
<h1 align=center><b><i>Hey!!! Look at my dad when he
  first wakes up in the morning!!!</b></i></h1>
<img src="images/sillydad.gif">
</body>
</html>
```

Note that "images/sillydad.gif" tells the computer to go to the "images" subfolder and open the file "sillydad.gif." Figure 3.3 shows the result.

**Figure 3.3. A Web page containing an image.**

Now try the same thing using an image file you have saved in your "images" folder.

# Positioning Images and Combining Them with Text

Now that you've managed to put an image on a Web page (it wasn't too hard, was it?), let's do something a bit more complicated. Let's say we have three images that we want to put on a Web page with some text by each picture. (By the way, to make my three pictures, I scanned one picture of my dad, which I called "dad1.gif." Then I copied this file twice, and renamed the copies "dad2.gif" and "dad3.gif." Finally, I used Microsoft Paint to draw on the copies.)

For our first try, use this HTML:

```
<html>
<head>
<title>3Dads</title>
</head>
<body>
These are three pictures of my handsome dad!
<img src="images/dad1.gif">
<img src="images/dad2.gif">
<img src="images/dad3.gif">
</body>
</html>
```

Figure 3.4 shows what we get.

Several things are not quite the way we wanted them to look. First, the images are next to each other. (If we made the Web page bigger, all three would be on the same line.) Second, the text, "These are three pictures of my handsome dad!" is positioned in an odd place and doesn't look very good.

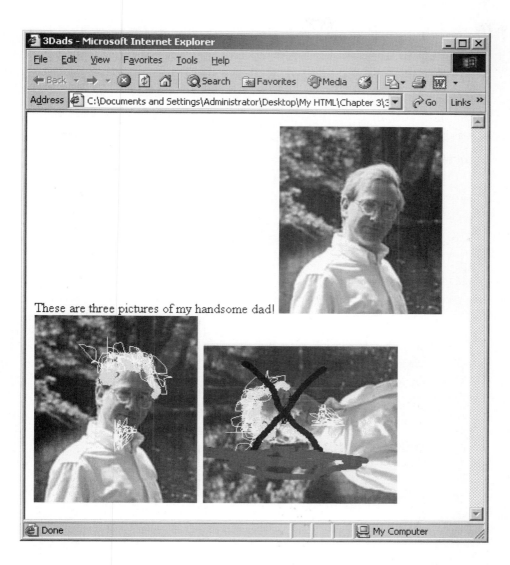

Figure 3.4.  A Web page with three images that aren't where we want them.

There's a reason why this happened that's kind of interesting and kind of stupid. HTML "thinks" an image is just like a single character, such as an "a" or "b." So it puts the first image right after the ". . . handsome dad!" text, then the next image right after that, and the third image right after that. Just like with text, when the images don't all fit on the same line, the browser wraps them down to the next line.

If you were paying attention in Chapter 2, you might think of using the break (**<br>**) tag. Yes, you would be right; that would put each image on its own line. But we're going to introduce another tag here, called the "rule" tag.

It looks like this: **<hr>**, and stands for "horizontal rule." (*Rule* means line.) It has no end tag. The rule tag is sort of like a break or paragraph tag, except that it puts a line across the page, making a nice, handsome break. You can use it anywhere you want to make a new section.

So, let's add an **<hr>** tag before each **<img>** tag, and furthermore, let's make the first text a nice, big header. Here's the HTML to do this, and Figure 3.5 shows the result in your browser:

```
<html>
<head>
<title>3Dads</title>
</head>
<body>
<h1>These are three pictures of my handsome dad!</h1>
<hr>
<img src="images/dad1.gif">
<hr>
<img src="images/dad2.gif">
<hr>
<img src="images/dad3.gif">
</body>
</html>
```

## ℹ CHECK IT OUT!

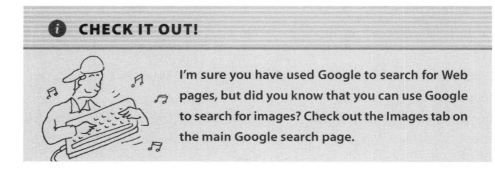

I'm sure you have used Google to search for Web pages, but did you know that you can use Google to search for images? Check out the Images tab on the main Google search page.

This looks much better, but we're still not done. Let's add some text next to each image:

```
<html>
<head>
<title>3Dads</title>
</head>
<body>
<h1>These are three pictures of my handsome dad!</h1>
<hr>
<img src="images/dad1.gif">
Here he's about age 45.
<hr>
<img src="images/dad2.gif">
Here he's age 48 - note the disappearing hair and scraggly
    beard. He blames these changes on my becoming a
    teenager.
<hr>
<img src="images/dad3.gif">
Here the burden of raising me has proved too much and
    he's become weirded out and needs a nap. Ha! Ha!
</body>
</html>
```

Now, when we look at the page in our browser, we get Figure 3.6.

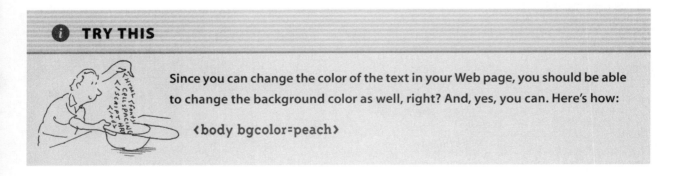

## ℹ TRY THIS

Since you can change the color of the text in your Web page, you should be able
to change the background color as well, right? And, yes, you can. Here's how:

```
<body bgcolor=peach>
```

Figure 3.6. Text added
next to each picture,
with the middle text
wrapping under the
image.

# These are three pictures of my handsome dad!

Here he's about age 45.

Here he's age 48 - note the disappearing hair and scraggly beard. He
blames these changes on my becoming a teenager.

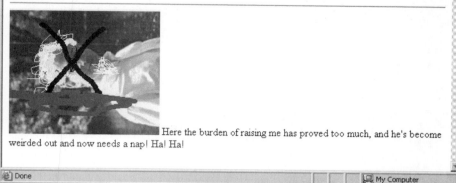

Here the burden of raising me has proved too much, and he's become
weirded out and now needs a nap! Ha! Ha!

Once again, we notice a problem: the text for the middle picture wraps
under the picture. Again, that's because HTML thinks of the image as a great
big character, so the text just wraps around it when there's no more room on

a line. Later, we'll learn about tables, which are the only good way to fix this. In the meantime, we'd be best off putting a paragraph (you remember, "`<p>`") before each line of text, and making all the picture captions level 2 headings (`<h2>`). Then we can use the center tag to center all the images and all the text at the same time.

```
<html>
<head>
<title>3Dads</title>
</head>
<body>
<h1>These are three pictures of my handsome Dad!</h1>
<hr>
<center>
<img src="images/dad1.gif">
<p>
<h2>Here he's about age 45.</h2>
<hr>
<img src="images/dad2.gif">
<p>
<h2>Here he's age 48 - note the disappearing hair and
    scraggly beard. He blames these changes on my
    becoming a teenager!
</h2>
<hr>
<img src="images/dad3.gif">
<p>
<h2> Here the burden of raising me has proved too much,
    and he's become weirded out and now needs a nap. Ha!
    Ha!</h2>
</center>
</body>
</html>
```

And now we're done, as you see in Figure 3.7. (But note that this Web page is now so long that we can't display it all on one screen. Later in this book, we'll show you how to add links that take you down to other parts of the page.)

Figure 3.7. Centering the entire page and making the text headings to improve the appearance.

# Making an Image the Background of Your Web Page

This is so easy it's almost ridiculous. Remember the body tag that looks like this: **<body>**? Try this:

```
<body background="images/dad1.gif">
<font color=white>
<h1>THIS IS UNSPEAKABLY HIDEOUS!</h1>
```

Here's what happens: The image is repeated in both directions (up and down and side to side) as needed to fill the background of your Web page. Figure 3.8 shows what it looks like using my dad's picture. (This would be good for my dad's fan club, if he had one!)

### ⓘ CHECK IT OUT!

To find out what colors are available in HTML, use Google to search for a phrase like "HTML colors."

# Making Text Flow Around an Image

What we did before, giving each picture of my dad its own caption, is the kind of thing you'd do for a photo album. But what if you wanted to make the image part of the Web page and have the text wrap around it? It turns out that you can use the "align" tag to do this. Here's a quick example, where the beginning letter *I* is an image:

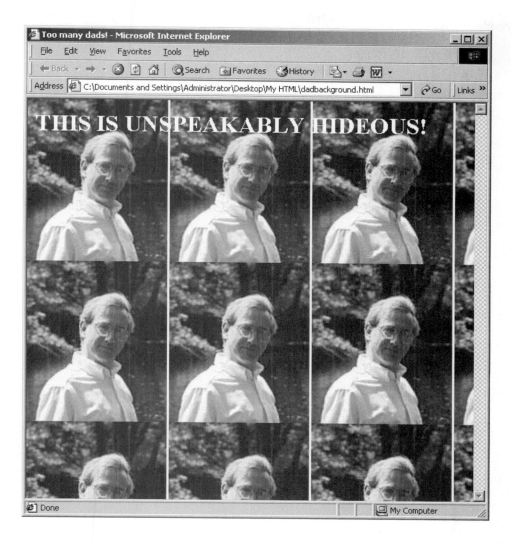

Figure 3.8. Using an image as a Web page background.

```
<html>
<head>
<title>Font1</title>
</head>
<body>
```

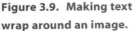

```
<img src="images/i.gif" align=left>
n the wild woods of Watchung, New Jersey, there lived a
    small <font face="Impact" size=5 color=purple>
    squirrel</font> named Ziggy. He was a happy squirrel,
    partly because he lived in the woods near the Selfridges.
    They were very nice to him and always fed him
    chocolate-covered acorns (his favorite) and everything
    was wonderful until Ben Selfridge decided that it would
    be fun if Ziggy could be trained to be his servant.
    Dressed in a black tuxedo, Ziggy was now put to work
    bringing Ben birch beer and cupcakes, potato chips and
    spring water, and other . . .
</body>
</html>
```

**Figure 3.9. Making text wrap around an image.**

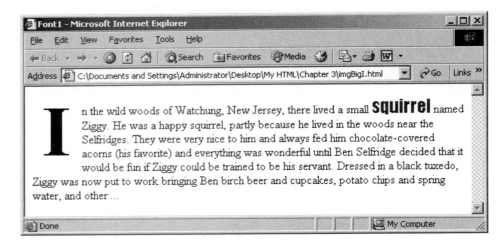

INTERESTING IMAGES

# Summary

In this chapter we went far beyond working with mere text and explored how to put images on your Web page. First, we described a little bit about how images are actually stored on a computer, and then we built a simple Web page with an image using the `<img>` tag. Next we explored the process of putting three images on a single page and discovered that we need breaks in the form of rules between them. Then we demonstrated two other cool things: using an image as the background for a Web page and getting text to wrap around an image.

# Challenge Questions 🔍

1. We used Microsoft Paint to create the little image of the capital *I* in Figure 3.9. Try doing this with another letter, and try to make the background of the image match the background in your Web page.

2. We also used Paint to rotate the third dad image in Figure 3.7. Can you see how?

3. Experiment with different colors for your Web page background and text. Which ones work well together?

# 4

# Likeable Lists and Terrific Tables

## Making Your Page Look Really Cool

**THIS CHAPTER WILL**

→ show you how to make text look nice by putting it into several varieties of lists;

→ introduce tabular data and show you what this is good for;

→ redo the images of my dad so the text is beside each image.

## Creating and Using Lists

Let's take an example from Chapter 2, where we created the beginnings of an online journal. Here's just the part that lists the assistant coaches; Figure 4.1 shows the resulting Web page:

```
<html>
<head>
<title>Asst.coach.list</title>
</head>
<body>
<h3>Assistant Coaches:</h3>
Susan Griffin
<br>
Peter Selfridge
<br>
Thomas Kirk
<p>
</body>
</html>
```

**Figure 4.1. List of assistant coaches set up with breaks.**

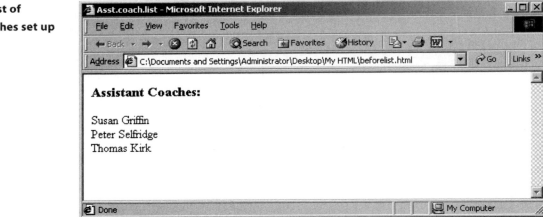

Although this Web page is perfectly readable, you can make it look better using lists. The simplest kind of list in HTML is the unordered list (<ul>). All you have to do is to start the list with a "<ul>" tag, then start each line of the list with a "<li>" ("list item") tag. This method is nice because it requires fewer tags and looks much better than the method we used in Figure 4.1. Here's the HTML, and Figure 4.2 shows the resulting Web page:

```html
<html>
<head>
     <title>Asst.coach.list</title>
</head>
<body>
<h3>Assistant Coaches:</h3>
     <ul>
          <li>Susan Griffin
          <li>Peter Selfridge
          <li>Thomas Kirk
     </ul>
</body>
</html>
```

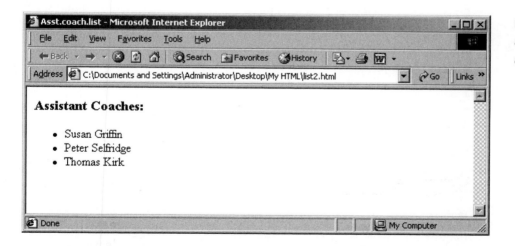

**Figure 4.2. List of assistant coaches set up as an unordered list.**

Isn't that cool? Note how we indented the HTML code. We think this looks really nice and the added structure makes the code more readable.

Here's another way to make a list: an ordered list (`<ol>`), which numbers the list entries. Figure 4.3 shows how it looks.

```
<html>
<head>
    <title>Ben's foods</title>
</head>
<body>
<h3>My favorite foods, from most to least favorite:</h3>
    <ol>
        <li>Pizza
        <li>Pancakes
        <li>Dad's delicious snack plates
        <li>Popcorn
        <li>Chocolate-chip cookies
        <li>Carrots
        <li>Dad's overcooked steak
        <li>Virtually any leftovers
        <li>Dirt
    </ol>
</body>
</html>
```

### ⓘ TRY THIS!

If you know how to use Microsoft Word, use it to create a simple list like the one we just made. Then save it as a Web page and see how it looks. Also check out the source. After a bunch of boilerplate, you can find the actual list HTML at the bottom. Compare this with our HTML.

And here's how it looks:

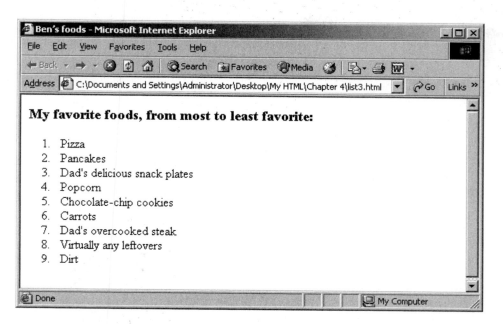

Figure 4.3. An ordered list.

You can do many other things with lists. For example, if you don't like using regular numbers (1, 2, 3, and so on) for the numbers, you can change them to letters or even Roman numerals! To do this, you add **"type="** to the **<ol>** tag. For example:

**<ol type=A>** will use A, B, C . . .

**<ol type=a>** will use a, b, c . . .

**<ol type=I>** will use Roman numerals: I, II, III, . . .

**<ol type=i>** will use lowercase Roman numerals: i, ii, iii . . .

Why would anyone want to use Roman numerals in a list? Well, it might make sense if you make lists inside of lists (called "nesting"). Then, you can make an outline in the style you were probably taught in school. (Note that each **</ol>** tag will turn off the most recent list you started.) Here's a little example (see also Figure 4.4):

```html
<html>
<head>
<title>Ben's favorite things</title>
</head>
<body>
<h3>Ben's favorite things:</h3>
<ol type=A>
<li>Favorite Video Games
    <ol type=1>
    <li>PlayStation
    <ol type=a>
    <li>Chronocross
    <li>Splinter Cell
    <li>Grand Theft Auto - Vice City
    </ol>
    <li>XBox
    <ol type=a>
    <li>Halo
    <li>The Getaway
    </ol>
    <li>Computer
    <ol type=a>
    <li>Diablo II
    <li>Quake II
    <li>Black and White
    </ol>
</ol>
<li>Favorite foods
</ol>
</body>
</html>
```

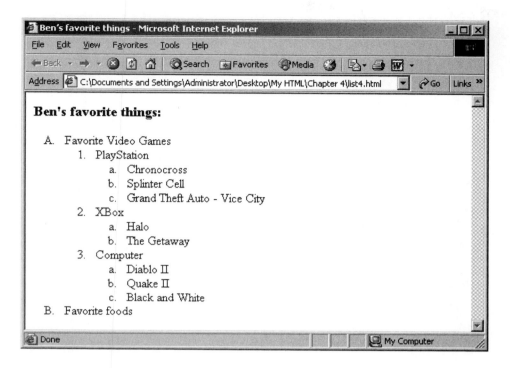

**Figure 4.4. Using nested ordered lists to create an outline style.**

# Creating and Using Tables

Let's go back to the online journal we created in Chapter 2. Remember the list of team players? We listed them in one column down the page. What if we wanted to list them in two columns, to save space on the page and make it look better? If we tried to do this by hand, it would be hard to make the columns line up. An easier and better way is to put the names in a table. Here's the HTML, and Figure 4.5 shows the resulting Web page:

```
<html>
<head>
<title>Table of Team Players</title>
</head>
<body>
<table border cellpadding=10>
    <caption><h2>Team members</h2></caption>
    <tr>
        <td>Ben Selfridge</td>
        <td>Tom Chagall</td>
    </tr>
    <tr>
        <td>Fred Murskinski</td>
        <td>Bob Barlett</td>
    </tr>
    <tr>
        <td>Kelly Mi</td>
        <td>Michael Jennings</td>
    </tr>
    <tr>
        <td>Eric Kestler</td>
        <td>Arthur Stevens</td>
    </tr>
    <tr>
        <td>Brayden Kirk</td>
        <td>Lohn Graden</td>
    </tr>
    <tr>
```

```
            <td>Loren Terveen</td>
        </tr>
    </table>
    </body>
</html>
```

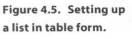

Figure 4.5. Setting up a list in table form.

**Table of Team Players - Microsoft Internet Explorer**

File  Edit  View  Favorites  Tools  Help

Back · → · ⊗ ⚲ ⌂ | ⚲Search ⭐Favorites ⚲History | ⤵· ⚛ ⚟ ·

Address ⚟ C:\Documents and Settings\Administrator\Desktop\My HTML\table1. ▾ | ⭮Go | Links »

## Team members

| | |
|---|---|
| Ben Selfridge | Tom Chagall |
| Fred Murskinski | Bob Barlett |
| Kelly Mi | Michael Jennings |
| Eric Kestler | Arthur Stevens |
| Brayden Kirk | Lohn Graden |
| Loren Terveen | |

Done                                    🖳 My Computer

So, what's going on here? Well, we made the list caption ("Team members") a heading because it looks much better that way. We started out with a **‹table›** tag with some attributes. (We've talked about adding attributes to tags before; for example, on page 34 we used the **‹h1›** tag and added an "align" attribute to center the heading. We also just used the "type" attribute with lists. Go back to page 53 and check it out.) Here we put in the border attribute, which draws lines to separate the cells of the table, and a cellspacing attribute set to 10. This adds more white space around each name so the table doesn't look cramped.

Then, we define each row of the table with the **‹tr›** tag, which is easy to remember as "table row." Between each pair of **‹tr›** and **‹/tr›** tags, we put each table element (or cell) between a **‹td›** and **‹/td›** tag. We think of **‹td›** as standing for "table data."

Let's try one other thing with tables, then you can use the Challenge Questions to explore them yourself. Remember in the last chapter when we put pictures of my dad on a Web page? The caption would start next to the picture, then wrap underneath it, so we put in rules and set up the text as headers. (Go back and look at Figures 3.6 and 3.7 if you want a reminder.) It turns out that you can put an image in a table just as easily as you can text. So let's use the same HTML code we used in the last example to re-create our page of dad pictures with the images in the left-hand cells and the text we wanted in the right-hand cells. That will make the text line up side by side with the images the way we wanted. Here's the HTML, and Figure 4.6 shows the resulting Web page:

```
<html>
<head>
<title>3Dads</title>
</head>
<body>
<table border>
    <caption><h1>These are three pictures of my
```

```
        handsome Dad!</h1></caption>
        <tr>
            <th><img src="images/dad1.gif"></th>
            <th><h2>Here he's about age 45.</h2></th>
        </tr>
        <tr>
            <th><img src="images/dad2.gif"></th>
            <th><h2>Here he's age 48 - note the disappearing
            hair and scraggly beard. He blames these
            changes on my becoming a teenager!
</h2></th>
        </tr>
        <tr>
            <th><img src="images/dad3.gif"></th>
            <th><h2> Here the burden of raising me has
            proved too much and he's become weirded out
            and needs a nap. Ha! Ha!</h2></th>
        </tr>
    </table>
    </body>
    </html>
```

### ⓘ CHECK IT OUT!

Poke around on the Web until you find what looks like
a list. Look at the source and see if you can find the list
tags.

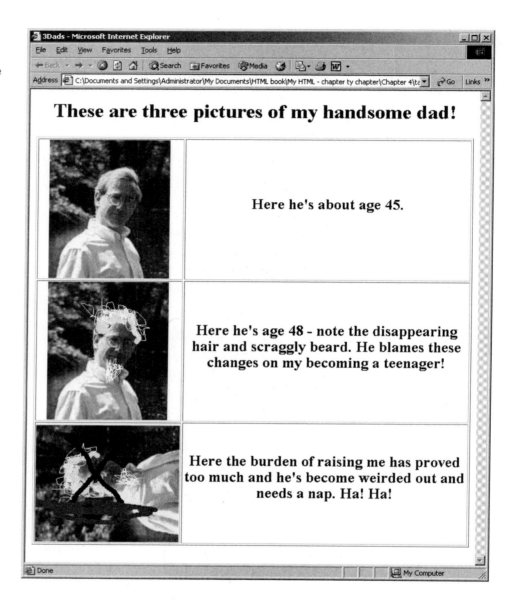

Here we used an alternative to the table data **<td>** tag. Instead, we used **<th>**, which stands for "table heading." This formats the text as a heading and centers it as well. We think putting the images and text into a table looks much better than what we did in Chapter 3. Also, it really shows how tables can let you put things side by side and then do whatever you want with each side.

## Summary

This chapter added to your knowledge of HTML by explaining lists and tables. We showed you how to create a few different kinds of lists, including a nested list that looks like an outline. Then we explored tables by taking part of the journal we created in Chapter 2 and making it into a more compact table. Finally, we put the pictures of my dad into a table so we could put the images and captions side by side.

## Challenge Questions 🔍

① Write the table of contents of this book as an HTML list with any style of headings you like.

② Create a table with three columns instead of two.

③ Reformat your journal from Chapter 2 using lists.

④ Take the table of team members we created in Figure 4.5 and see if you can center it.

⑤ Take the last table we did, with images and text side by side. See if you can switch the middle picture and its text (so the text is on the left and the image on the right).

# The Really Fun Stuff

# 5

## Using Links to Design a Complete Web Site

## Adding Links to Other Pages

**THIS CHAPTER WILL**

→ show you how to link one Web page to another page you've created;

→ explain anchors and anchor links that link to different parts of the same Web page;

→ show you how to make a link to any page on the Web;

→ provide examples of image links;

→ show you how to design and build a complete, multipage Web site.

Finally, we're going to talk about what made the Web what it is today—hypertext links, or links for short. A link is a mouse-sensitive piece of a Web page. (As you'll see, it's usually text but can also be an image or even part of an image.) If clicked on, it will bring up a new Web page in your browser or move the browser to another part of the current Web page.

I'm sure you've heard of a *URL,* which stands for universal resource locator. A URL is simply the address of a page on the Web (a document, really, but that's not an important distinction right now), like "www.yahoo.com," "www.zephyrpress.com," or "www.html-for-kids.com." The reason why the Internet is called the World Wide Web is because Web pages have links connecting them to other Web pages, which themselves have links, and so on. So the entire Web is really a huge, interconnected set of pages. Now let's learn how to put a link into one of your Web pages. First, let's create a new page of links to some of the Web pages you've already made using this book.

Let's say your "My HTML" folder looks like Figure 5.1. (This is what our folder looks like at this point in the book.)

**Figure 5.1. Contents of our "my HTML" file.**

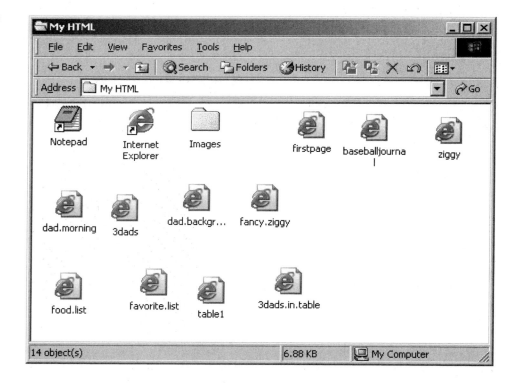

Let's create a new Web page that has links to two pages in this folder. We'll start by copying "firstpage.html" and renaming it "mypages.html." (You know how to do this by now.) Then edit the new file in Notepad so it looks like this. We are going to examine the new code carefully:

```
<html>
<head>
    <title>My pages</title>
</head>
<body>
The first page I created was simple. All it said was <a href=
    "firstpage.html">hello world</a>. But it was cool anyway.
<br>
My second page used breaks, paragraphs, and headings to
    make a journal about my <a href="baseballjournal
    .html">baseball game</a>.
</body>
</html>
```

Let's look at the most important line in this HTML. It starts with the <a> tag, has a "href=" part (attribute, right?), some text (the "hello world") and

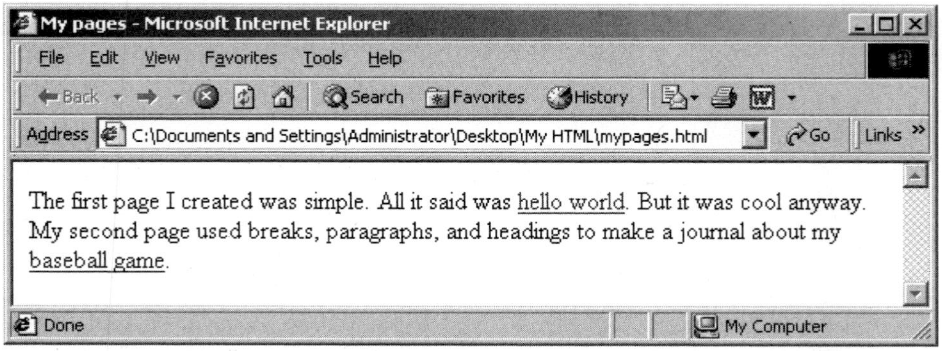

**Figure 5.2. Simple links to documents on the same computer.**

then ends with the **</a>** tag. The "**<a>**" says, essentially, "I want to make a link." The "**href=**" is then followed by the URL of the link, in this case, "first-page.html," the page you already made that is in your folder. The text "Hello, World" forms the link to "firstpage.html."

The link, "hello world," is displayed in the Web page in a special way. In our browser it shows up underlined (and in a different color, but you can't see that here). So the new page looks like Figure 5.2.

If you move the mouse over the "Hello, World" link, the cursor will turn into a little hand, and if you click on the link, the browser will display your first Web page. Likewise, if you click on "baseball game," you'll get your journal page.

There are two things to note here. First, if you want to display the linked Web page in a new browser window, you can right-click and select "Open Link in New Window." Second, if you don't do this, you will have to use the browser's "Back" button to return to the previous Web page.

The URL we used in this example is called a *local URL,* meaning it's the address of a Web page on the same machine. When you link to a local URL, you need to specify the path to the file you're linking to. (In this case, since the file is in the same folder, you don't need a path.) But if the file were in another folder, you'd have to include that folder's name in the path. It turns out you've already done this! In the last chapter, when you put all your images into the "images" folder, then placed an image in your Web page, you used "images/dad1.gif" because the file "dad1.gif" was in the "images" folder.

If you want to add a link to another page on the Web, the command looks exactly the same except for the URL. Here's an example, and Figure 5.3 shows how it looks in your browser.

```
<html>
<head>
<title>Favorite links</title>
</head>
```

```
<body>
<h2>Here are some of my favorite links:</h2>
    <a href="http://www.disney.com">Disney</a>
    <br>
    <a href="http://www.html-for-kids.com">HTML For
    Kids</a>
    <br>
    <a href="http://www.google.com">Google</a>
    <br>
    <a href="http://www.zephyrpress.com">Zephyr
    Press</a>
<br>
</body>
</html>
```

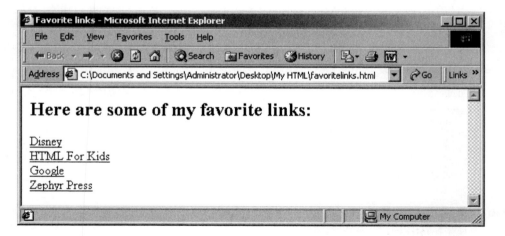

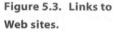

**Figure 5.3. Links to Web sites.**

# Adding Image Links

Adding an image link is simplicity itself, once you know how to add an image and make a link. As an example, I have a Web page named "dadbio.html," which contains a short biography of my dad. I also have an image of my dad called "dad1.html." I can make the image link to the bio page like this:

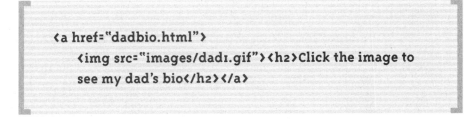

```
<a href="dadbio.html">
    <img src="images/dad1.gif"><h2>Click the image to
see my dad's bio</h2></a>
```

You see, whatever is after the "<a href= . . .>" command becomes the active link. In this case, both the image and the words, "Click the image to see my dad's bio," are links and will bring up the "dadbio.html" page. Figure 5.4 shows how the Web page looks:

**Figure 5.4. Examples of image and text links.**

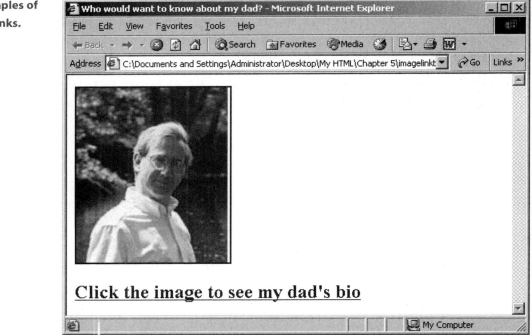

THE REALLY FUN STUFF

We hope you can see that the browser has put a border around the image, indicating that it is a link. (If you don't like the border, you can add the attribute "**border=0**" to the image [**<img>**] tag, and that will get rid of it.) Figure 5.5 shows what you'll get if you click on either the image link or the text. (Here we assume you right-click and select "Open Link in New Window.")

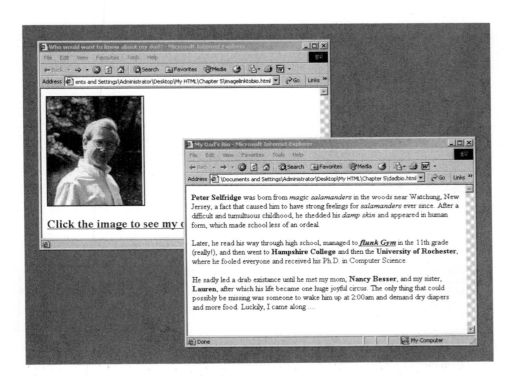

**Figure 5.5. The linked document opened in a new window.**

# Adding Links to Different Parts of the Same Web Page

Adding links that point to different parts of the same Web page is also easy, but it involves two steps. The first step is to make an *anchor* in your Web page (we think of it as being like a bookmark) using the name attribute. This attribute names a section, or anchor, so you can put that name into a link.

Since we haven't created a really big Web page yet, we'll just give you a simple example of the idea here. Let's pretend you've expanded your baseball journal (the one you made in Chapter 2) to describe five games you've played. You've chosen to keep all the descriptions on one page. (We'll discuss decisions like this in the next section.) Now you want to add a sort of table of contents to the page, with links so people can go to whichever game they want to read about. What you do is make an anchor at the beginning of each game. Here's what that would look like for a couple of games:

```
<h3><a name="Game 1">Game 1</h3>
<p>
[Lots of awesome text describing the game would go here.]
<h3><a name="Game 2">Game 2</h3>
<p>
[Lots of awesome text describing the game would go here.]
```

What have we done here? It's so easy it's almost silly. We've created a heading for Game 1 and one for Game 2. We named them using the **<a>** tag and the name attributes "Game 1" and "Game 2." Now, at the top of the page, we can make our little table of contents that refers to these anchors with this HTML:

```
<body>
<a name="Top">
<h2>Table of Contents (click to go to each game)</h2>
<ol>
    <li><a href="#Game 1">Game 1</a>
    <li><a href="#Game 2">Game 2</a>
</ol>
```

What have we done here? We've made a heading ("Table of Contents") then a basic ordered list. You should remember this from Chapter 4 (see page 52). For each list entry, we've added an **<a href= . . . >** tag followed by the name of the anchor with a "#" before it, all in quotation marks. (Why, you ask, does it need a "#" before it? The answer is we don't know, and you shouldn't care. You just have to use it.)

What this does is to turn each list element into a link to the corresponding anchor. So if you click on the link, the browser will take you straight to the anchor. Let's take the concept one step further and do what many Web pages do: add another anchor and link that bring you up to the top of the

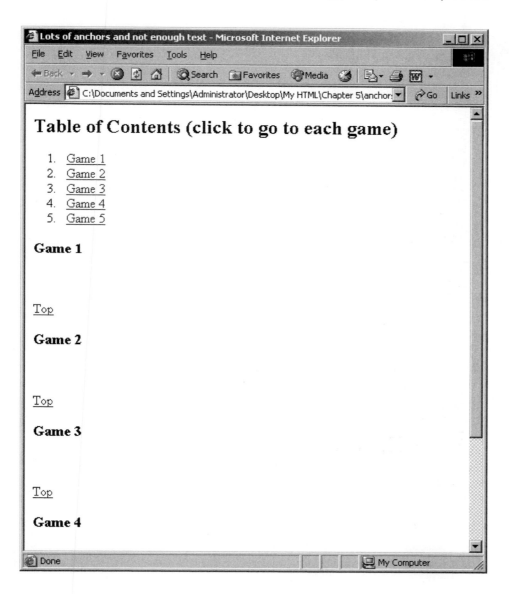

Figure 5.6. Examples of links to navigate down a page and back to the top.

page again. Here's the framework for five games, and Figure 5.6 shows the resulting Web page (or part of it anyway).

```html
<html>
<head>
<title>Lots of anchors and not enough text</title>
</head>
<body>
<a name="Top">
<h2>Table of Contents (click to go to each game)</h2>
<ol>
    <li><a href="#Game 1">Game 1</a>
    <li><a href="#Game 2">Game 2</a>
    <li><a href="#Game 3">Game 3</a>
    <li><a href="#Game 4">Game 4</a>
    <li><a href="#Game 5">Game 5</a>
</ol>
<h3><a name="Game 1">Game 1</h3>
    <br>
    <br>
    <a href="#Top">Top</a>
<h3><a name="Game 2">Game 2</h3>
    <br>
    <br>
    <a href="#Top">Top</a>
<h3><a name="Game 3">Game 3</h3>
    <br>
    <br>
    <a href="#Top">Top</a>
<h3><a name="Game 4">Game 4</h3>
    <br>
    <br>
```

THE REALLY FUN STUFF

```
        <a href="#Top">Top</a>
    <h3><a name="Game 5">Game 5</h3>
        <br>
        <br>
        <a href="#Top">Top</a>
    </body>
    </html>
```

If you look at the links in your browser, you can see they are a different color. If you click on a link in the table of contents, the browser will go to that game. If you click on any of the "Top" links, the browser will go to the top of the page again. We think this is really cool, and so should you!

---

### ℹ DID YOU KNOW?

Search engines like Google (there are a bunch of others) work by actually creating an *index* of the Web. They do this using computer programs that "crawl" over the Web following all possible links.

---

# Overall Web Site Design

The last (and quite probably the most important) aspect of Web design we need to introduce is making links to your own Web pages. If you've used the Web at all, you are surely aware of how useful these little nuggets of power can be. No detailed Web site can consist of a single page. That means all the pages have to be structured and organized to make it easy for whoever's visiting to navigate your site. Links are the key to making this happen.

Mapping out your Web site is extremely important in making it fun and interesting to visit. It's also one of the most basic processes ever to exist in the computer world. In Figures 5.7 and 5.8, we've given two examples of how to map out a Web site. The arrows represent links from one page to the next, and everything in a rectangle is a page or subpage.

**Figure 5.7. Mapping a Web site.**

**Figure 5.8. Mapping a Web site.**

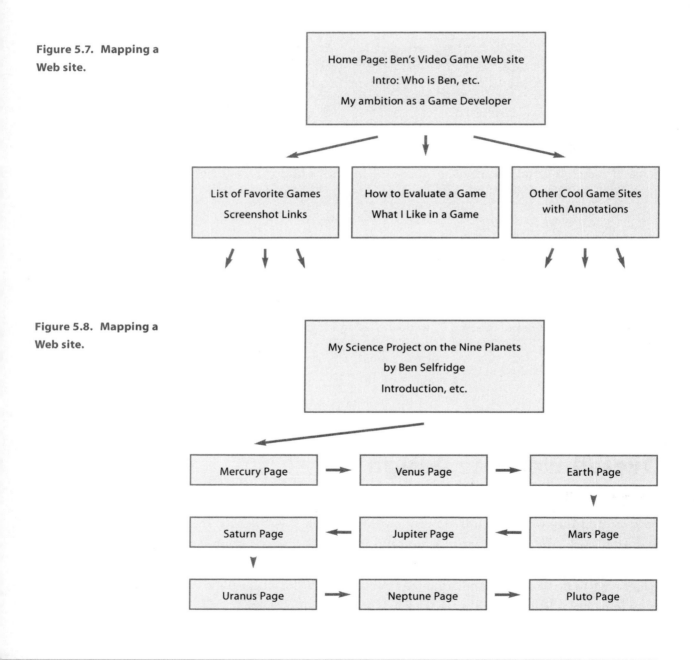

These are two classic designs used all over the place, but you can come up with something original and exciting if you think they're too bland. Maybe you want to have some kind of navigation system on the screen all the time, such as a bar on the left. Or perhaps you'd prefer to use images as links. Whatever you come up with is great, as long as it works and is not tedious to the person who's visiting.

Once you've developed a map of what you want on the pages and how they're linked, the next step is to design each page. Depending on the purpose of your Web site, you may want each page to have a similar style, or as is sometimes said, a similar "look and feel." The reason for a consistent design is to give your visitors an intuitive sense of where they are. Of course, this is easier said than done unless you're a professional Web designer. But you can take some simple steps that will help:

→ Select a nice background color and use it on all your pages.

→ Select a nice and readable font (and a color that goes with the background) and use that for most, if not all, of your text.

→ Lay out each page so that it is simple to view: not too crowded, and obvious in its intent.

These simple guidelines will go a long way toward making a pleasing Web site.

# Building a Web Site from Several Pages

So let's actually build a Web site from some of the pages we've created. Let's say the purpose of the Web site is to show someone the work that you've done, or maybe this is just part of your personal Web site.

Let's take the folder of pages we showed in Figure 5.1 and use that directly in our design. The folder we showed actually had the Web pages in three handy rows more or less corresponding to the Web pages we developed during

Chapter 2 (Fun with Fonts), Chapter 3 (Interesting Images), and Chapter 4 (Likeable Lists and Terrific Tables). So let's imagine a main page with links to each of these pages, as in Figure 5.9.

**Figure 5.9. Graphic showing links from a main page to all the Web pages we've created.**

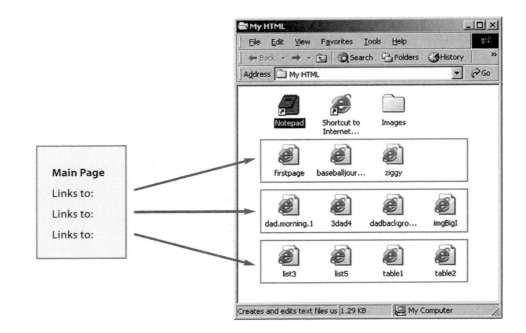

So, how do we want the main page to look? Let's sketch out a rough design, shown in Figure 5.10.

What will the HTML look like? Well, we're really hoping that by now you could do this yourself! And we bet you can! Here are a few tips, then we'll do the actual link section as a table:

→ The title will be a level 1 heading (you remember, **<h1>**).

→ The biography, description, and picture will be a table with one row and two columns, and the second column will have an image in it.

→ The links will be in a table with three rows and multiple columns.

So, how are we going to set up the table of links? Well, let's use lists in the second column of each table row, and each list will be a list of links to the pages you've created. Indenting your HTML really helps here:

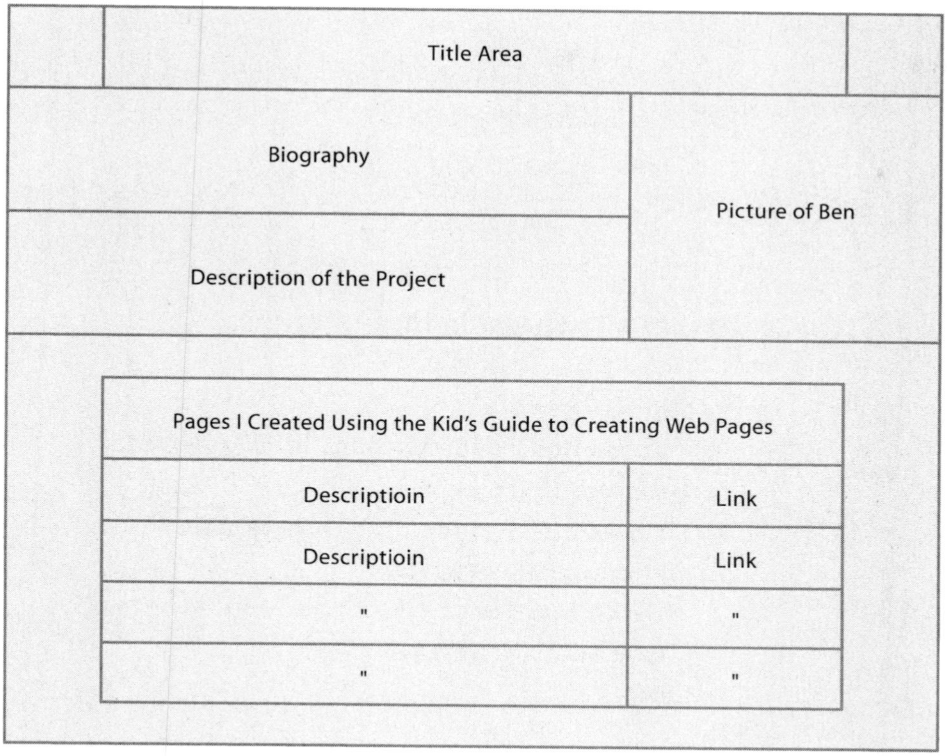

**Figure 5.10. Rough design of the main page.**

| Title Area | |
|---|---|
| Biography | |
| | Picture of Ben |
| Description of the Project | |

| Pages I Created Using the Kid's Guide to Creating Web Pages | |
|---|---|
| Descriptioin | Link |
| Descriptioin | Link |
| " | " |
| " | " |

```
<table border cellpadding=5>
<caption><h2>Web Pages I Created Using<i>A Kid's
Guide</i></h2></caption>
<tr>
     <td>Mainly Text Pages</td>
     <td>
        <ol>
           <li><a href="firstpage.html">Hello,
           World</a>
           <li><a href="baseballjournal.html">
           Baseball Journal</a>
```

```
                    <li><a href="ziggy.html">Ziggy in a
                    Different Font</a>
                </ol>
            </td>
    </tr>
    <tr>
        <td>Pages with Images in Them</td>
        <td>
            <ol>
                <li><a href="dad.morning1.html">My Dad in
                the Morning</a>
                <li><a href="3dad4.html">Three More
                Pictures of My Dad.</a>
                <li><a href="dadbackground.html"><b>Don't
                look at this!</b></a>
            </ol>
        </td>
    </tr>
    <tr>
        <td>Pages with Lists and Tables</td>
        <td>
            <ol>
                <li><a href="list3.html">My Favorite
                Foods</a>
                <li><a href="list5.html">Other Favorite
                Things</a>
                <li><a href="table1.html">Baseball Players in
                a Table</a>
                <li><a href="table2.html">My Dad's Pictures
                in a Table</a>
            </ol>
        </td>
</table>
```

Figure 5.11 shows how it looks. Each list item on the right is a link to a page you created. Isn't this cool?

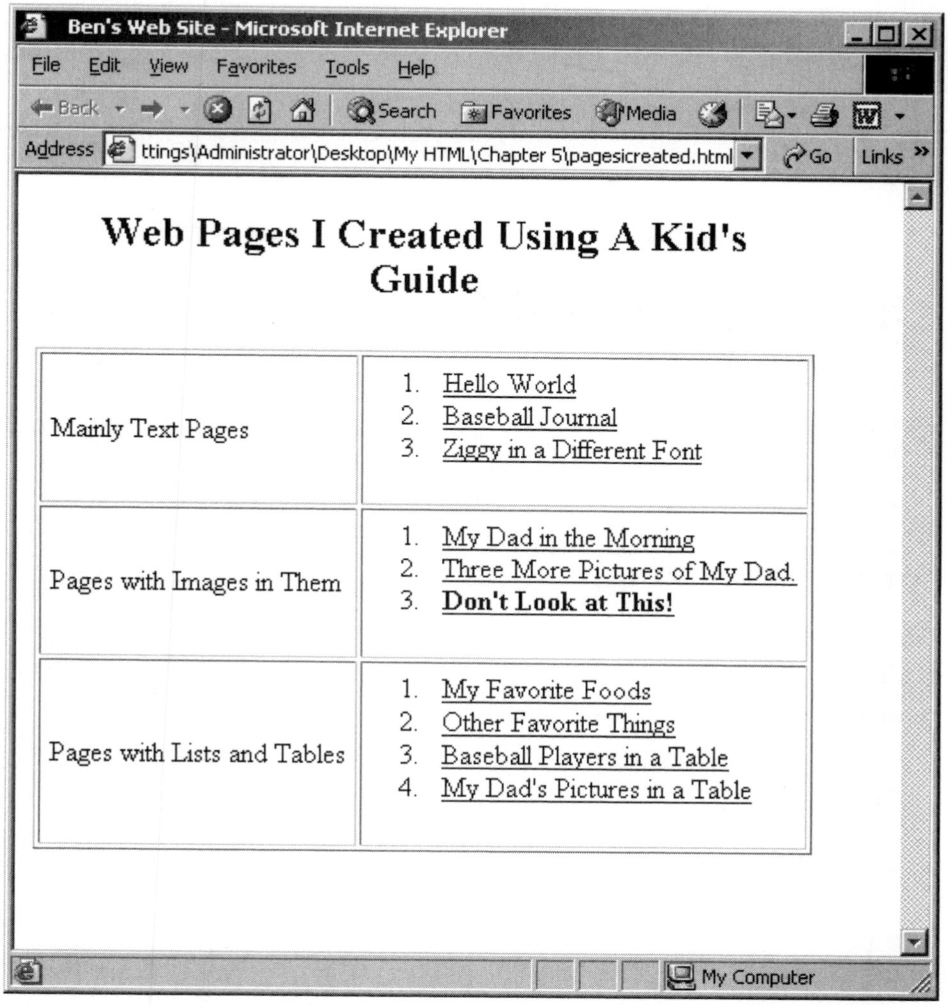

Figure 5.11. Links set up in table format.

## Summary

We started this chapter with a brief discussion of URLs and links, making a simple page that linked to two other pages we'd already made and stored on our computer. Then, we made some links to Web sites on the Internet and showed you how to make an image into a link. (How cool is that?) Making links from one section to another of the same page is pretty easy too: all you have to do is to define anchors and use the anchors in your `<href>` tag. Then we switched gears a bit and talked about different ways to organize a Web site and design a Web page. Finally, we made a page that put links inside a table.

## Challenge Questions 🔍

**❶** What happens if you click on a link that doesn't point to a valid Web page? Has that ever happened to you before?

**❷** Go to a Web page you're familiar with and look at the source. Can you find the links in the source?

**❸** Use the example in Figure 5.11, but see if you can make the links in a nested table (that is, a table within the cell of another table) inside the right-hand table cells. This looks pretty neat.

# 6

# Publishing Your
# Work on the Web

## Showing the World
## What You Can Do

## Introduction

Hey, fooling around learning HTML on your computer is fine, but if you actually want other people to see your work, you have to publish it. By publish it, we mean putting it on a Web server on the Internet. So, we're going to take this opportunity to tell you a bit about how the Web works. (Just a little bit, so don't worry!)

The Web, or Internet, is a network of computers linked together. Some computers are *Web servers,* which means they can provide Web pages to other computers hooked up to the Internet. Each Web server has an address called an *Internet protocol* (IP) address, which is a twelve-digit number written like this: 123.987.456.654. Luckily, you don't have to remember any IP addresses because there's a way of mapping URLs to their IP addresses. This means you and your computer can use "www.zephyrpress.com" instead of the site's twelve-digit number. (Of course, if you knew the twelve-digit number, you could actually type that into your browser.)

When you start your browser and type in a URL, your computer sends a message over the Internet to the Web server that corresponds to that URL. (The protocol, or "language," it uses is called HTTP, which stands for Hypertext Transfer Protocol. This is why URLs start with "http://," although you can almost always leave that off now.) If you click on a link, the computer usually sends a message with a URL followed by some other information that tells the Web server what page you want. The Web server then finds the page you requested and sends it back to your computer, and your browser then displays it. That's pretty much all there is to it!

# Organizing and Checking Your Work

The first step toward publishing your HTML on a Web site is to create your Web pages on your computer. You can do that with what you've learned in this book. In this book, we've also shown you a couple of ways to organize Web pages, as well as how to put things like images into their own separate folders and, in general, keep everything as organized as possible. The bottom line is to make sure everything works exactly the way you want it to on your computer. Only when you are sure you've worked the bugs out should you plan on publishing your pages to a Web site.

# Steps in Publishing Your Web Pages

Lots of Web hosting companies will allow you to publish your Web pages on their Web server for free (at least if the pages are not too large), and we recommend this as a first step. Unfortunately, they do insist on putting advertisements on your page, but hey, they have to make money somehow! We aren't going to recommend a particular site, because it might be out-of-date by the time you read this book. Instead, we suggest you go to Google or another search engine and type in "free Web site" or something like that. You should have no problem finding a place to publish your work.

Once you've made sure everything works on your computer and have picked a place to publish your Web site, the rest is easy. Basically, all you need to do is to follow their directions to upload your files (all the HTML files you've built, including directories or folders that hold images).

There's one thing we didn't tell you yet that may be important. There's a convention that your *home page,* the first page displayed when people visit your site, is called "index.html." We're not sure why that is, but if you put your stuff on the Web, you may have to rename your home page. No big deal, obviously.

Once you've loaded your stuff on the Web, you'll want to follow every link and visit every page to make sure everything works right. Again, if you've already checked everything once on your computer, this step should be easy.

# Further Steps

You may already know this, but you can register your own domain name (www.yourname.com), as long as the name is not already taken. Once you've registered a domain name, you "own" it for a period of time (such as a year). Registering costs a modest fee (well, depending on how much money you have), somewhere around $35.00. The outfit that registers your domain name for you will also be very happy to host your Web site (although not for free) and sell you additional services such as email and stuff like that. We registered "www.html-for-kids.com" for this book, and the process was really pretty easy.

# Summary

This chapter briefly explained how to take the HTML Web pages you developed on your own computer and put them on the Web using a Web hosting company. Many companies will host your site for free but will put advertisements into your Web page. Before publishing, the most important thing to remember is to check your work carefully and completely understand what you've done. If you've done this, uploading your files so they appear correctly on the Web should be pretty straightforward.

## Challenge Questions 🔍

❶ See if your name is registered as a domain name. First try to go to "www.yourname.com" and see what happens. If you don't reach a Web site, go to a site that allows you to register domain names and see if your name is available.

❷ Use the web pages you've built using this book to design your own Web site. First, sketch out your site as we've shown you, then actually build it!

❸ Publish your pages on the Web. Tell your friends!

# 7

# A Little Bit of JavaScript

## The Power of Programming

### THIS CHAPTER WILL

→ show you a very easy and cool addition to a Web page called an alert;

→ explain a little bit about JavaScript, which is a real programming language;

→ show you some neat things you can do with JavaScript;

→ we hope, get you interested enough to start learning JavaScript on your own!

## Jump Right in with Alerts

Let's jump right in with a simple example of JavaScript. Create a file called JavaScript1.html with the following HTML in it:

```
<html>
<head>
    <title>My first little JavaScript</title>
    <script language="javascript">
        alert ("Are you aware that you are visiting the
        Web site of a very cool person?");
        alert ("Well, now you know!")
    </script>
</head>
<body>
<p>
<h1>I'm sure glad we got that out of the way!<h1>
</body>
</html>
```

Now run the file in your browser and see what happens. You should get
two alerts, one after the other. The first will say, "Are you aware that you are
visiting the Web site of a very cool person?" and the second, "Well, now you
know!" Each will stay up until you click the "OK" button. Then, when you click
the second "OK," the Web page will open with "I'm sure glad we got that out
of the way!" as a heading. Figure 7.1 shows what the first alert looks like:

**Figure 7.1. Example of an alert.**

Pretty cool, huh?

# JavaScript: What's It About?

*JavaScript* is a computer language that allows you to write computer programs that run as part of your Web page. HTML is a computer language, too. But, as you now know, it is pretty much limited to describing how a Web page looks. JavaScript can do much, much more. One way it is often used is to check data entered into a Web page. (We're going to do that in the next JavaScript example.) But it can also do almost any kind of computation there is. It really is a general-purpose computer language.

Unfortunately, we're not going to talk much about JavaScript, only show you some tricks you can use to make your Web page more fun. Learning JavaScript is a great idea, and we really recommend it. Just like with HTML, the best way to learn JavaScript is to get a book, sit down at the computer, and do it.

So, let's go back to the example we just gave. What's going on here? Let's repeat the important lines:

```
<script language="javascript">
    alert ("Are you aware that you are visiting the Web
    site of a very cool person?");
    alert ("Well, now you know!")
</script>
```

First, we used the **<script>** tag to start a script section, and we specified that we were going to use JavaScript as our language. Then we put in two JavaScript alert commands. Since you ran your JavaScript1.html in your browser, you should have a really good idea what an alert command does. Basically, it pops up a little text box with a message in it. Further, it pretty much forces you to read the message because nothing else will happen until you hit the "OK" button. In this case, after you click "OK" on the first alert, a second alert pops up. Only after that is "OK"-ed is the rest of the Web page displayed. Alerts are kind of fun, but they're also pretty intrusive. If you put those two alerts inside a Web page you wanted people to visit often, you'd be surprised (or maybe you wouldn't) how quickly people would get tired of them. For this reason, use alerts sparingly and for good reasons. What might a good reason be? Check out the next example.

# Entering and Checking Input to a Web Page

You know, so far all we have shown you is how to display information in a Web page. But you know from using the Web yourself that you are often asked to enter information. How is this done? Rather than talk about it abstractly, let's look at an example:

```
<html>
<head>
    <title>My second little JavaScript</title>
    <script language=javascript>
function CheckForReasonableAge() {
    age = window.prompt ("How old are you?")
    if (age == 13)
        alert ("Wow! How cool is that! That's my age!")
    else
    if (age < 5)
        alert ("That's too young! I don't believe you!");
    else
    if (age > 95)
        alert ("That's too old! I don't believe you!")
```

```
        else
            alert ("Hmmm. OK. I guess that's interesting.")
        }
        </script>
    </head>
    <body>
        <INPUT
TYPE=button value="Click on this"
onClick="CheckForReasonableAge()">
    </body>
    </html>
```

Don't freak out! It's not that complicated! We'll explain every piece of this. But before we do, why don't you enter it into a file called "JavaScript2.html" and try running it in your browser? You should get a Web page with a button, and if you click on it, a little form should pop up that looks like Figure 7.2 (my dad actually entered his age into the form).

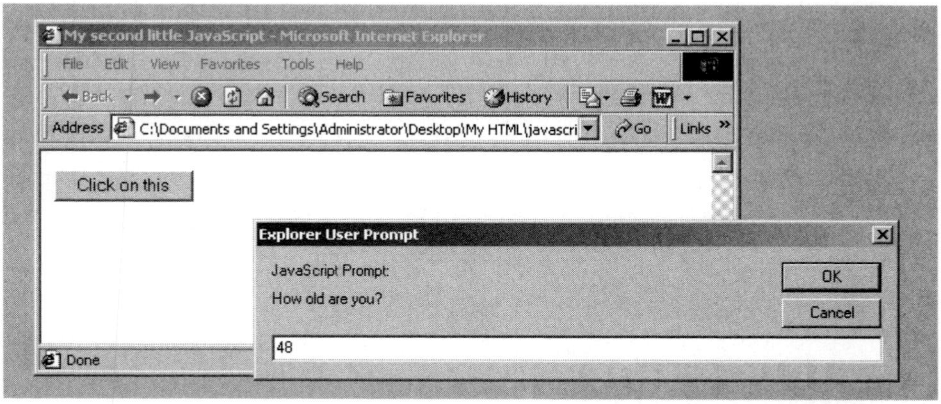

Figure 7.2. Entering information into a Web page.

Now try entering different numbers in the little box and hitting "Enter" Try the numbers -55, 3, 5, 13, your age, and iiiiii. Then look back at the Java-Script code. You'll probably begin to get the idea what this code does right away. But "getting the idea" is not enough. Let's really try to understand the code. There are two obvious parts, the script part and the body. Let's look at the body first.

The body starts with an **<INPUT>** tag with three attributes, one of which is special. **<INPUT>** means that the Web page is going to ask the user for some input (duh!). The attribute "Type" specifies that the input is going to be a button and the value is simply the label that appears on the button. Then comes the special attribute. What this says is simply, "When the button is clicked, 'call' or 'go to' the function 'CheckForReasonableAge.'" This means that the Web page starts to execute, or run, the code called "CheckForReasonableAge" in the script part of the page.

The script part describes what is called a function, and the name of the function is "CheckForReasonableAge." A function is simply some code that does not run automatically (as the alerts did) but has to be called using its name. We'll explain more about this in just a minute.

So when you enter an age into the form and hit "Enter," the CheckForReasonableAge function is called and is "given" the form. The function CheckForReasonableAge gets the actual age you typed using the 'age = window.prompt ("How old are you?")' statement and uses that to do three comparisons. If you read "==" as "is equal to," "<" as "is less than," and ">" as "is greater than," you should be able to understand the code.

This is an odd example—probably not something anyone would want to do. But how might you use this type of code? Well, have you ever had to register for something and enter your email address on a Web page? You might have noticed that if you enter your address incorrectly (without an "@," for example) the Web page will complain (often with an Alert). This is almost certainly done with JavaScript.

# List of Squares

JavaScript is much more powerful than these examples—in fact, it's a real programming language with variables and loops. Here's one more simple example:

```
<html>
<head>
<title>for loops</title>
<script language="JavaScript">
    for (i = 1; i <= 25; i++) {
        j = i*i
        document.write (i + " squared is: " + j + "<br>")
    }
</script>
</head>
</html>
```

Type this code into a file named JavaScript2.html, and give it a try. You should get Figure 7.3.

So what's happening here? The first new idea here is that of a *variable*. Here, this JavaScript uses two variables: *i* and *j*. You can think of a variable as a little envelope that can hold a value. In particular, the "envelope" *j* is set equal to *i\*i*, which means "*i* times *i*," or *i* squared. (We actually used a variable called "age" in the last example.)

The second new idea is that of a loop. A *loop* is a way of running a bunch of JavaScript commands again and again. We've used a *for loop*, which is probably the most popular kind. The for loop uses another variable called "*i*," and here's what it does. First, it sets *i* equal to 1—that's the "*i*=1" part. Then it checks to make sure that *i* is less than or equal to 25. If it isn't (that is, if *i* is 26 or higher), it stops the loop. If it is (which it will be for a while, especially since we've just set *i* equal to 1), it executes what is between the curly brackets {}. Then it adds 1 to *i*—that's the "i++" part. (The "++" is called an *operator* because it operates on the variable *i* by adding 1 to it.) Does this make sense? Finally, it shouldn't surprise you that "document.write" writes to the Web page, and can write both text (what is between the quotation marks) and the value of a variable. So instead of writing "*i*" on the page, it writes *i*'s value.

If you look at the code carefully, then look at the output, you should figure out the gist of this. See the Challenge Questions to test yourself.

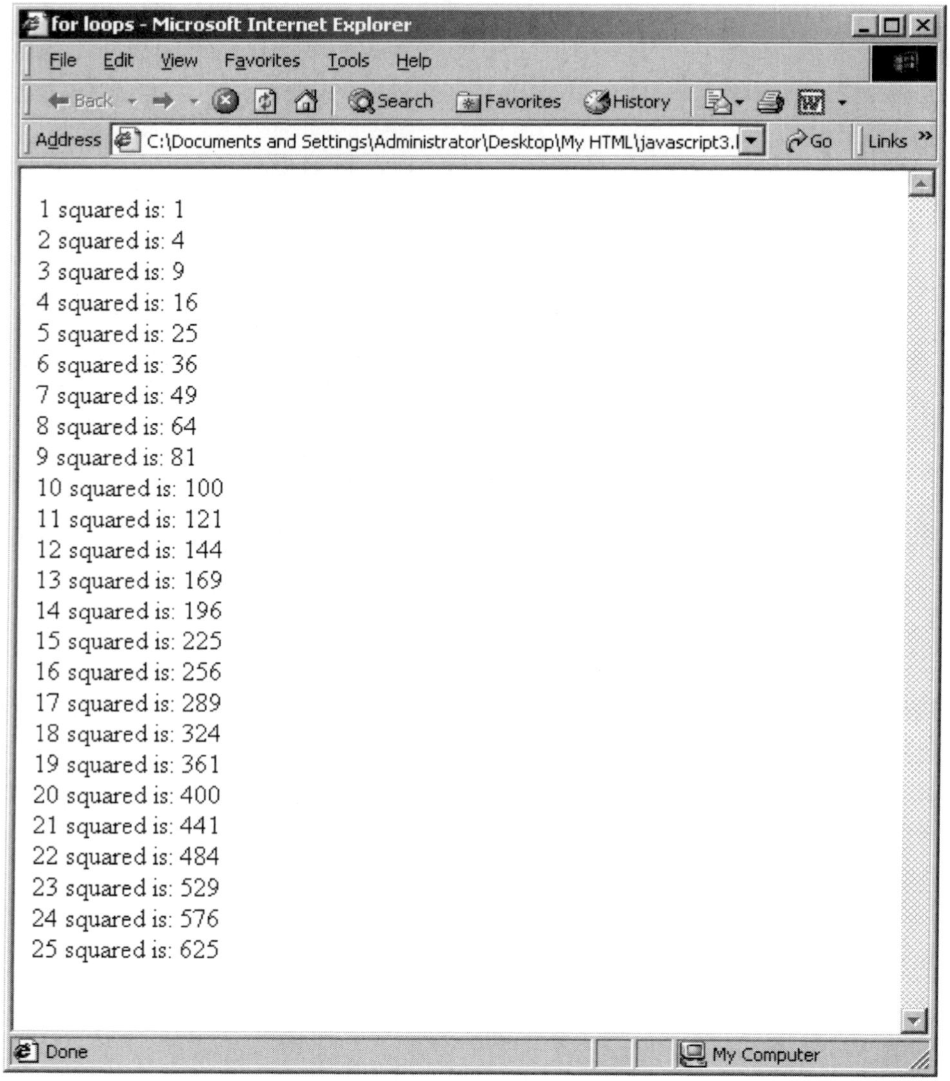

**Figure 7.3. A function for finding mathematical squares written using JavaScript.**

```
for loops - Microsoft Internet Explorer

File   Edit   View   Favorites   Tools   Help

Back                Search   Favorites   History

Address  C:\Documents and Settings\Administrator\Desktop\My HTML\javascript3.    Go   Links

1 squared is: 1
2 squared is: 4
3 squared is: 9
4 squared is: 16
5 squared is: 25
6 squared is: 36
7 squared is: 49
8 squared is: 64
9 squared is: 81
10 squared is: 100
11 squared is: 121
12 squared is: 144
13 squared is: 169
14 squared is: 196
15 squared is: 225
16 squared is: 256
17 squared is: 289
18 squared is: 324
19 squared is: 361
20 squared is: 400
21 squared is: 441
22 squared is: 484
23 squared is: 529
24 squared is: 576
25 squared is: 625

Done                                    My Computer
```

## Summary

This chapter has shown you a little bit of JavaScript. Unlike in previous chapters, we don't really expect you to do much more than study the code and our explanations and understand them as best you can. You probably won't be able to write much original JavaScript on your own at this point. Of course, feel free to experiment as much as you like.

## Challenge Questions 🔍

❶ Try making your own alerts. They are fun.

❷ Change the JavaScript program we showed you so that it prints out not only the squares of the numbers from 1 to 25, but also their cubes.

# 8

# Conclusion

## What's Next?

### THIS CHAPTER WILL

→ briefly describe a few other cool things you can look forward to learning about if the stuff in this book grabs you;

→ remind you to *have fun!*

## Introduction

My goodness, what's next? If we're not careful, we could write another book in this chapter! There is so much more you can do with HTML, and learning HTML leads you to learn many other fun things as well. So we'll have to restrain ourselves. We'll just briefly talk about style sheets, which are really important. Then we'll tell you some other nifty things about HTML and a few other cool Web technologies, some of which I (Ben) have been playing around with.

In this chapter, you'll see several exciting things, including a little about *cascading style sheets* (or CSS, for short) and other HTML things that are a little more advanced. Now, since this book is specifically a tutorial introduction to HTML, we (unfortunately) cannot go into very much depth. Please enjoy this chapter! We hope it will tickle your fancy enough to make you pursue more knowledge (perhaps in a future book by us).

# Cascading Style Sheets and DHTML

Although HTML is fun to play around with and is useful for creating Web pages, it's not exactly versatile. That is, it is often frustrating because it won't do what you want in terms of positioning items on the screen, choosing font color, and many other features. Meet CSS. CSS is kind of complicated, so we're just going to mention it. This amazingly nifty tool allows Web designers (that's you) to define the color, position, font type, and everything (yes, everything) else you could possibly want for a text or image.

CSS can do two different things:

1. It can allow you to redefine a tag, such as **‹h1›**, to do something else. (For instance, it could make the text between the tags red or really big.)

2. It can allow you to define whole new sets of properties that you can use later in your HTML.

In fact, if you combine CSS with JavaScript (that mutant language featured in Chapter 7) and something called the Document Object Model (DOM), you get what is called Dynamic HTML (DHTML). Again, that's another acronym that sounds really complicated, but in fact, it isn't. (We've always thought that the computer world sounds too complicated for its own good.) With this ingenious system and a good understanding of JavaScript and CSS, you can change and animate objects on the screen. If we produce a future book, it will most definitely have detailed explanations of how to use CSS to your mischievous advantage.

# Frames

Have you ever seen a Web page that was divided into different sections? These might include a navigation bar on the left, a title at the top that is separated from the rest of the page, and the content in the middle section. All of these sections are called *frames*. Each one is actually a separate Web page, merged in the final *frameset* (basically all of the pages put together, which is what the visitor sees). In fact, if you select "View" on the bar at the top of your screen, then select "Source" or "View Source" to see the HTML code behind the page, you will see something like this:

```
<html>
<head>
    <title>Some Sort of Title</title>
</head>
<body>
<frameset cols="110,*,110">
<frame src="nav.html" name="1navigation">
<frame src="content.html" name="content">
<frame src="photos.html" name="pictures">
</body>
</html>
```

Here, the sources for all the different frames are "**nav.html**," "**content.html**," and "**photos.html**." Now, we're going to do something cool with this information. See the text box at the top, by the other options, that contains the URL of the page? Highlight everything after the very last "**/**" in it. For instance:

```
http://www.mygennies.com/genny1/pictures.html
```

Delete this part, then type in "**nav.html**," or one of the other pages you saw in the source of the original page. Press "Enter," and you will see that frame standing by itself in the screen! Some pages have JavaScript that will protect you from seeing one frame by itself, but many coders overlook that step, allowing you to see in turn the code they used to make each frame!

# Other Cool Web Technologies and Applications

We'd like just to mention some other cool Web technologies and applications that you might be interested in learning about:

**FLASH** → Flash is a system for creating and displaying animations on the Web. A company called Macromedia created it. If you've ever seen cartoon-like animations on the Web, they were probably created using Flash.

**IM** → IM stands for "Instant Messenger," and we'd be really surprised if you haven't heard of it—in fact, you probably use it! This nifty application lets you "chat" with your friends and other people on the Web, send files and other kinds of information, and keep handy buddy lists. It will even tell you when a "buddy" is logged on and can be contacted!

**BLOGS** → This is a relatively new kind of Web content. "Blog" stands for "Web log," and it's a way to rapidly publish short pieces of text. Blogs have become remarkably popular.

**JAVA** → Java is a full-fledged programming language that is more complicated than JavaScript and is used to create Web content. You use Java to create what is called a "Java Applet" that can run in your browser.

**XML** → XML is supposed to be a replacement for HTML, but it doesn't seem to have caught on as fast as people expected it to. XML allows you to create your own tags and define what you want those tags to mean.

# And This Is the End

Well, that's the end of this chapter and our book. We thank you very much for reading it and hope you enjoyed it. Please feel free to visit our Web site (www.html-for-kids.com) and let us know by email what you thought of it. Remember:

**HAVE FUN!**

# Glossary

**APPLICATION** → An application is something that can run on your computer, like Microsoft Word, Internet Explorer, or a game like Solitaire.

**ATTRIBUTE** → An attribute is an additional and optional piece of information added to a tag that further defines the formatting (appearance) of the Web page. For example, the **‹p›** tag makes a new paragraph. Adding the align attribute **‹p align = center›** will center the paragraph.

**BROWSER** → A browser, or Web browser, is the application (or program) that you use to display Web pages on your computer. The browser is responsible for taking a URL, going out on the Internet, finding the site associated with the URL, sending a request for the Web page to the site, receiving HTML in return, and then interpreting the HTML to create the Web page you see. There are several different Web browsers, but Internet Explorer and Netscape Navigator are probably the most popular.

**DESKTOP** → The desktop is simply the screen you see on your computer after you start up. It includes the taskbar at the bottom and a number of icons (little pictures) for different applications and folders. You can change the appearance (and other characteristics) of the desktop by right-clicking on an empty part of it. That will bring up a set of interesting tabs you can play around with.

**DOMAIN NAME** → A domain means a specific part of the Internet (determined by the IP, or Internet Protocol, address, which we won't go into here). What it means non-technically is that part of a URL that comes after the "www." So, for Zephyr Press, the domain name is "zephyrpress.com" and the domain name for this book's Web site is "html-for-kids.com." (*See also* URL.)

**EXTENSION** → All the information on your computer is stored in named bundles called files. Traditionally, files, especially those that hold information for an application, have a name and an extension separated by a period, like "mypaper.doc," "firstpage.html," or "shoppinglist.txt." The ".doc." ".html." and ".txt" are the file name extensions. Your computer often uses the extension to figure out which application to use to open the file (as well as which icon to use to represent the file). Typically, ".doc" indicates a Microsoft Word file, ".html" means your Web browser, and ".txt" means Microsoft Notepad. You can right-click on a file icon and select "Properties" to see a file's extension. (*See also* file.)

**FILE** → As we describe under "Extension," information on your computer is stored in named bundles called files, and a file usually has a name and extension. You double-click on the icon for a file to open that information. (*See also* extension, icon.)

**FONT** → *Font* has a remarkably complicated technical meaning dating back to when books and manuscripts were printed using letters on little pieces of lead that had to be framed and lined up and inked and then pressed onto the paper. But its approximate meaning is the kind of text used in an application, like Word or Notepad, used for creating documents. A font has a face, or typeface, like Arial or Times New Roman, that specifies how the letters look, and a size, like 12-point.

**HOSTING →** Hosting means using a Web server to make someone's Web site visible to everyone on the Internet. There are lots of outfits that will host your Web site (your collection of Web pages) under your domain. It's actually possible to do this yourself on your home computer. But it really only makes sense to host your own site if your computer is on and connected to the Internet all the time.

**HTML →** Hypertext Markup Language, the language used to specify how Web pages look.

**HTTP →** Hypertext Transfer Protocol. Once upon a time (not all that long ago, actually) when you typed a URL into your browser, you had to put "http://" before the "www" part. This would tell your browser that it should use HTTP as the language to ask for and receive the HTML for the page you wanted. There are other languages, or protocols, that run on the Internet, but HTTP is by far the most common and relevant to most people. Now most browsers automatically use HTTP if you just type in the "www . . ." part of the address. (*See also* URL.)

**HYPERTEXT →** Hypertext is a word invented early in the computer era that means, roughly, "text with links in it." Once upon a time, before HTML was created, there were a number of different hypertext systems. Any of these would allow you to read text on your computer and click on a link in the text to go to another part of the document or another document (or file) all together. HTML pretty much dominates now, because it's used on the World Wide Web. (*See also* HTML.)

**ICON →** An icon is a little graphical image (a picture) that represents files or applications on your computer. Typically, a file with a certain extension will show up with a particular icon that makes it recognizable, so all Word documents (extension: .doc) will have the same icon, a blue *W*. (*See also* extension.)

**IMAGE FILE** → A file on your computer that contains an image, which is a (usually large) set of numbers that describes the color of each pixel in the image. Image files typically have ".bmp," ".gif," or ".jpg" extensions, although there are many more image formats available. Because image files tend to be large, you should be careful if you try to send images as email attachments. (*See also* pixel.)

**INTERNET** → The Internet is a vast, worldwide set of computers hooked together with wires. The wires used to be regular phone lines (yes, the computers on the Internet once had to "call each other" to connect). But now they are typically high-speed wires. The Internet is connected so that there are different ways to get from one computer to another. That way, if one way is blocked or too busy, the communication can take another route. The Internet supports email and browsing, among other things. It is the basis for the World Wide Web, in sort of the same way that roads are the basis for automobile driving.

**JAVA** → Java is a powerful, general-purpose programming language. It was developed in part to run as part of a Web page, as a so-called "applet." It is used in a lot of places both on the Web and off. Java is *not* the same thing as JavaScript (*see also* JavaScript).

**JAVASCRIPT** → JavaScript is a computer language that is written as part of a Web page (as you'll learn in this book). Using it you can do a number of cool things. It's a real programming language.

**LINK** → *See* hyperlink.

**NOTEPAD** → Notepad is a simple Microsoft word-processing application. Its big brother is Microsoft WordPad, and the head of the family is Microsoft Word. We use Notepad in this book to show you how to create Web pages.

**PIXEL →** Pixel stands for "picture element" and means a small dot that is part of a picture. Inside an image file, a pixel is one or several numbers that tells the computer what color that dot of the picture is. If the picture is 400 by 400 pixels, then in theory we need 160,000 numbers. Thus, image files are typically very big. However, some picture formats (like GIF and JPEG) compress the file to a much smaller size.

**SEARCH ENGINE →** A search engine is a Web application (that is, an application you get to by visiting a Web page). It can search the Web for information you give it. Google is our favorite search engine.

**TAG →** A tag is an HTML formatting command, the basis for creating Web pages. You can recognize tags because they are inside angle brackets ‹ ›. Usually, tags come in pairs, one to "turn on" the command and a second that starts with "/" to turn it off. There are many, many different tags (this book only scratches the surface) and many tags can have attributes. (*See also* attributes.)

**URL →** URL stands for universal resource locator, and it usually means the address of a Web page. You know, the old "www.whateverpageiwant.com." There's actually a bit more to a URL, but it really isn't important for this book.

**WEB BROWSER →** *See* browser.

**WEB PAGE →** A Web page is the basic display unit of the Web. This is what your Web browser shows you on your screen when you go to a Web site.

**WEB SERVER →** A Web server is a computer that hosts one or more Web sites. Typically, Web servers are fairly powerful computers that are (almost) always available and are connected to the Internet with high-speed connections and special software so that many people can visit the Web sites at once without the server getting bogged down.

**WEB SITE →** A Web site is a collection of Web pages that is hosted by a Web server and referenced by a URL. (*See also* URL, Web server.)

**WORLD WIDE WEB (WWW)** → The World Wide Web is almost the same as the Internet. But it really means that part of the Internet that uses HTTP and HTML to store and deliver Web pages. It was the invention of HTML that allowed the Internet to become the Web and really take off for all of us. (*See also* HTML, HTTP.)

# About the Authors

**B**ENJAMIN SELFRIDGE is a normal fourteen-year-old student in Warren, New Jersey. His outdoor interests include hiking and camping with his dad, Little League baseball, skiing, biking, and running around. Indoors, he can be found playing video games, reading, listening to music, doing magic tricks, and, of course, using the computer. In school, Ben plays the drums in both honors and regular band, and especially likes social studies, math, and lunch. When Ben was eleven, he became interested in creating Web pages and did a school project on the subject. His abilities have recently advanced to include some JavaScript programming with the help of his dad.

**P**ETER SELFRIDGE has a Ph.D. in computer science and worked at Bell Labs and AT&T Labs as a computer researcher for many years. He currently works for a science and engineering services company, and is a technology consultant on artificial intelligence. He has also given numerous talks on these subjects, as well as organizing and managing many workshops and conferences. More recently, he worked as the vice president of engineering and chief technology officer for a computer animation company, and as a technology consultant for an artificial intelligence company.

When not working, Peter enjoys being a parent to Benjamin and Lauren (his nineteen-year-old daughter), doing home repair, gardening, and playing acoustic guitar. He is also an avid backpacker and camper.

# Index

A2170 701151 0